Sisterly Networks

FRONTIERS OF THE AMERICAN SOUTH

UNIVERSITY PRESS OF FLORIDA

Florida A&M University, Tallahassee
Florida Atlantic University, Boca Raton
Florida Gulf Coast University, Ft. Myers
Florida International University, Miami
Florida State University, Tallahassee
New College of Florida, Sarasota
University of Central Florida, Orlando
University of Florida, Gainesville
University of North Florida, Jacksonville
University of South Florida, Tampa
University of West Florida, Pensacola

SISTERLY NETWORKS

Fifty Years of Southern Women's Histories

EDITED BY CATHERINE CLINTON

Foreword by William A. Link

UNIVERSITY PRESS OF FLORIDA
Gainesville | Tallahassee | Tampa | Boca Raton
Pensacola | Orlando | Miami | Jacksonville | Ft. Myers | Sarasota

25 24 23 22 21 20   6 5 4 3 2 1

Library of Congress Cataloging-in-Publication Data
Names: Clinton, Catherine, 1952– editor. | Link, William A., author of foreword.
Title: Sisterly networks : fifty years of Southern women's histories /
edited by Catherine Clinton ; foreword by William A. Link.
Other titles: Frontiers of the American South.
Description: Gainesville : University Press of Florida, 2020. | Series:
Frontiers of the American South | Includes bibliographical references and index.
Identifiers: LCCN 2020017094 (print) | LCCN 2020017095 (ebook) | ISBN
9780813066615 (hardback) | ISBN 9780813057620 (pdf)
Subjects: LCSH: Southern Association for Women Historians. |
Women—Southern States—History. | Women's studies—Southern
States—History. | Women—Southern States—Social conditions.
Classification: LCC HQ1438.S63 S57 2020 (print) | LCC HQ1438.S63 (ebook)
| DDC 305.40975—dc23
LC record available at https://lccn.loc.gov/2020017094
LC ebook record available at https://lccn.loc.gov/2020017095

The University Press of Florida is the scholarly publishing agency for the State University
System of Florida, comprising Florida A&M University, Florida Atlantic University, Florida
Gulf Coast University, Florida International University, Florida State University, New College
of Florida, University of Central Florida, University of Florida, University of North Florida,
University of South Florida, and University of West Florida.

University Press of Florida
2046 NE Waldo Road
Suite 2100
Gainesville, FL 32609
http://upress.ufl.edu

Contents

Foreword

Sisterly Networks: Fifty Years of Southern Women's Histories is the third volume appearing in the Frontiers of the American South series. Our purpose in this series is to explore topics that push our understanding of what makes (and has made) the American South. Further, Frontiers of the American South asks historians to consider different thematic approaches as well as new views about the historical meaning of the South, how it evolved over time, and the relevance of this evolution for our own time.

Sisterly Networks, which includes five essays by distinguished scholars in Southern women's history, celebrates a half century of the Southern Association for Women Historians (SAWH). The purpose of this volume is to reflect on the flood of scholarship about gender and the South, as well as the evolution of women in what was until the recent past a male-dominated profession. SAWH has been a critical incubator of new and dynamic scholarship, a successful advocacy group, and an important force for mentoring young historians.

My own experience with SAWH, as a young scholar, was equally positive and enriching. I began to attend the SAWH's annual meeting about thirty years ago, and a highlight of the Southern Historical Association has been the address by a leading scholar of women's history. Often these addresses offered an early peek at work in progress that later appeared in print. The SAWH was and is welcoming, supportive, and dynamic.

Meredith Babb and Sian Hunter of the University Press of Florida have been a part of this series since its inception and have provided indispensable assistance in helping us navigate book publishing. Both Meredith and Sian are exceptional editors, and we have greatly benefited from their skill.

The preparation of this volume involved efforts by a variety of people. Above all, Catherine Clinton organized and edited the writing of these essays with her usual skill, energy, and broad vision. The volume's contributors all worked diligently and punctually, and I appreciate their collegiality and common support for this project. The Milbauer Program in Southern History, at the University of Florida, has profited from the enthusiasm of graduate students Aurelia Aubert, Madison Cates, Anthony Donaldson, Meagan Frenzer, Lauren Spencer, and David Meltsner, who helped bring this volume to fruition. David, in particular, worked assiduously in supporting this project.

William A. Link
Series Editor

Introduction

CATHERINE CLINTON

The movers and shakers of women's history during second-wave feminism and particularly the women who in 1970 founded the Southern Association of Women Historians (named changed to Southern Association *for* Women Historians in 1985) would likely be surprised as well as delighted by current strides by feminist scholars and women historians in all fields, but particularly in Southern women's history. They doubtless would be amazed by how the Southern academy has adapted to female colleagues and feminist agendas. Coming together to celebrate fifty years of organizational outreach, mentoring and fundraising, prize-giving and programming, it is a good time not only to take stock of this organization but also to reflect on our academic enterprise: the challenges and accomplishments at half a century. The fluidity and dynamism of women's history has combined with important recognition of race and region within the American past, and twenty-first-century shifts take into account the dramatic acceleration of historical revisionism.

Certainly, many women were actively involved in the formation of the Southern Association for Women Historians (SAWH), as were men. This organization became an important crossroads for growing the field: organizing conferences, producing volumes, sponsoring book prizes, and, most importantly, storming the archives. A steady parade of researchers stopped begging for crumbs and began to make demands. These demands included marching right up to the front door, ringing the bell, and refusing to be denied entry.

Several generations later, a group of dedicated historians gathered at the University of Florida in Gainesville in November 2018 to debate and discuss the state of Southern women's histories at a conference highlighting the upcoming fiftieth anniversary of the Southern Association for Women Historians. Invited speakers were asked to take on issues personal and political and to comment on academic and intellectual trends, both great and small. This call to reflection was an attempt to capture some of the combustible and exciting developments within Southern women's histories and to celebrate the networks and sisterhood that a half century had fostered.

Participants ranged from past presidents of the organization, former officers and board members, editors of SAWH volumes, and a cadre of students (perhaps future leaders of the organization). We attracted independent scholars and endowed chairs, doctoral candidates and emerita professors, and the theme of inclusion permeated—as it has from the organization's earliest days.

Male privilege and female exclusion were pronounced throughout American higher education for most of the twentieth century, and this was particularly the case within the Southern academy. A dynamic generation of scholars challenged this conventional wisdom to become pathbreakers: women such as Julia Cherry Spruill, who wrote from Chapel Hill but outside the academy and in whose honor a book award is given annually by the SAWH; Willie Lee Rose, who was the chair of the Status of Women Committee of the American Historical Association that produced the "Rose Report" in 1970, who in 1977 was the first woman to hold the visiting Harmsworth Chair at Oxford University, and for whom a book award of the SAWH has been named; and Mary Elizabeth Massey, who arrived at Chapel Hill in 1939, secured a post at Winthrop College, and would become president of the Southern Historical Association (SHA) in 1972. When A. Elizabeth Taylor (after whom the SAWH named its annual essay prize) came to Chapel Hill in 1938 to enroll for her doctorate, she was the sole woman in the premier Southern graduate history program—until Massey arrived the following year. These two women were advised by a male faculty member that although women were "welcomed" to the program, at the University of North Carolina, "we don't do anything for them."[1]

Women began to do for themselves, and Southern women created a fairly strong track record during the second half of the twentieth century, exploiting bonds of sisterhood through collaborative efforts. And the field seems to be still going strong in the twenty-first century. First and foremost, the SAWH takes seriously trying to model behavior that provides best practices for members and rising generations.[2] Although the organization began with cochairs, the SAWH shifted very quickly into a system requiring that a nominating committee select a second vice president to rise through the ranks and serve as president for a one-year term of service (after serving as a vice president for two, essentially training on the job).

This system was suspended briefly during the 1990s, when a slate of two of more candidates was presented to the membership and put to a vote. These elections did not serve the organization well and were finally disbanded in favor of a single name being put forward by the nominating committee to insure that all potential leaders might be willing to serve the organization in a presidential capacity. The organization was growing, but it was not robust enough to withstand this electoral process. The SAWH continues to use a nomination system, which allows for write-in candidates, but seeks to support collective rather than competitive leadership.

Further, instead of asking each year's president to deliver an address, the SAWH president invites a scholar of his or her choice to offer a talk to the assembled attendees at the annual awards ceremony (see appendix B). Some former addresses have been edited into a volume, for the University of Missouri Southern Women series.[3] Again, a spirit of inclusion signals the SAWH's commitment to serve as many of our members as possible.

It has not been a completely smooth path, as the organization has stumbled more than once, making costly mistakes and missteps. When the organization presented its first Willie Lee Rose Prize to the 1987 publication of *Montgomery Bus Boycott and the Women Who Started It: The Memoir of Jo Ann Gibson Robinson,* the organization presented the editor of the volume, David Garrow, a white male scholar, with a plaque on the occasion of the award. The SAWH failed to honor the memoirist, Jo Ann Gibson Robinson, herself. This oversight caused embarrassment and consternation and created a cloud over the proceedings. Things could have been worse, but the membership was deeply disturbed by this mistake, and members struggled to bury the memory of this incident and to create an ethic to do better—extending itself when possible to create an improved climate of racial inclusion.

Despite the patriarchal nature of many Southern colleges and universities, Southern women seemed to negotiate the shoals with surprising skill on this issue of leadership. Larger national organizations, such as the American Historical Association (AHA) and the Organization of American Historians (OAH), lagged behind the SHA in securing top posts for women—particularly during the twentieth century. Although Nellie Neilson was nominated for president of the AHA in 1932, she wasn't elected until 1943, and it wasn't until the 1980s that a petition campaign put another woman on the ballot: Natalie Zemon Davis, who became only the second female president of this prestigious organization in 1987.[4] Although Louise Kellogg was elected president of the Organization of American Historians in 1930, it would be fifty years before another woman assumed the top spot: Gerda Lerner in 1981. During that period, the SHA elected three women presidents: Ella Lonn, Kathryn Trimmer Abbey Hanna, and Mary Elizabeth Massey.

Anne Firor Scott's SHA presidency in 1989 heralded a new era because Scott had taught for years at a prestigious Southern institution while publishing work in the field of Southern women's history. This was a significant turnabout, considering the less-than-warm welcome Scott received when she arrived in Chapel Hill, North Carolina, with a Harvard Ph.D. in the 1950s. She was told that the University of North Carolina had never hired a woman and never would. But when Harvard's Oscar Handlin told UNC department chair Fletcher Green to hire Scott, he did as he was told. Scott later recalled that her appointment was only part-time and she was denied an office (among other indignities), but she went on to join the faculty at Duke University in 1961 and to publish and promote Southern women's history.[5] She ended up with an endowed chair at Duke, and the SAWH established a mid-career prize in her name.

During the economic boom of the 1950s, Southern female scholars struggled alongside Northern sisters for token recognition, but often they resigned themselves to secondary status. The number of women receiving doctorates during this era went into precipitous decline.[6] Southern women might have grown complacent about subordinate roles, but larger stirrings within the culture began to question women's exclusion and to protest sexist stereotyping. Some of these protests encouraged female historians to band together to try to improve women's numbers among Southern history faculty—again, only through sisterly efforts could the sisterhood prevail. Members of an earlier generation, isolated and so few in number, may have disdained such tactics; keeping a low profile was, for them, a survival technique. Historian A. Elizabeth Taylor recalled that when Ella Lonn tried to organize a women's breakfast within the SHA, she received a cold shoulder because "the women weren't interested because many people felt that you shouldn't segregate yourself."[7]

During this era, with women just emerging from the shadows within the academy, there were interesting debates among teachers and scholars, historians and archivists, about how best to achieve advances for professional women within the field. Some advocates clearly favored feminist solidarity and seeking male allies, while many within these previously all-male bastions decided that becoming "one of the boys" and keeping any feminist tendencies under the radar was a better method of moving up the ladder. Then, of course, there were women who sought status and power within the profession without having to hide any feminist tendencies—quite simply because they didn't *have* any. There were many struggles on the path to advancement, and, indeed, clashing agendas among newly minted Ph.D.s in history.

Eventually a younger, perhaps more strident, and definitely more strategic group of feminists within Southern history departments determined that an organization would strengthen their positions in the "boys' club" atmosphere of the academy. Mollie Camp Davis, former chair of the History Department at Queen's University in Charlotte, North Carolina, was born during the Great Depression, and she, like many in her cohort, was determined to agitate for change and to bring about improvements in her lifetime. This generation's mothers had been the first group of women able to vote with the passage of the Nineteenth Amendment in 1920. They broke down barriers at institutions of higher learning by challenging the *glacial* pace of progress and by launching assaults on structural impediments that kept women from leadership opportunities.

And so it was that a vibrant group of women organized themselves into a caucus dedicated to promoting female historians within Southern institutions, and Southern women's history within historical fields, societies, and departments.

It was this double-barreled set of aims that struck a new chord within the field, as women's history was a nascent and even maligned field at the time. The caucus had its humble beginnings in November 1970 in a cubicle next to the boiler room in the basement of the Galt House Hotel in Louisville, Kentucky, where the Southern Historical Association was having its thirty-sixth annual meeting. This was the only space offered during the conference.

Decades later, the transformative empowerment of Southern women's history is on display—at the thirty years of SAWH conferences (tri-annual since 1988), the nine SAWH volumes (including conference proceedings and oral histories), and the collection of scholarly prizes—as members garner status within other organizations, as well as major awards.[8] Current developments reflect the maturation of the field, the escalating interest in Southern women's history, and the diversification both of American women's history, to reflect race and region, and of Southern history, to include gender and sexuality.

So many of these transformations reflect both the expansion of archival resources and the application of new methods to extract forgotten and neglected female historical experience, bringing gender issues out of the shadows. Indeed, in recent years, Southern women's history has come out of the closet as twenty-first-century scholars explore same-sex relationship and LGBTQIA (Lesbian, Gay, Bisexual, Transgender, Queer/Questioning, Intersex, and Asexual/Allied) issues.

Female membership in historical organizations has soared, along with representation on editorial boards and advisory committees and in other influential spheres. Many previous departments that were all male have been integrated by white women. Further, the presence of black women in these formerly white preserves supports welcome advances. A larger percentage of postgraduates in history are women, particularly at public universities. And some may want to echo the slogan, "you've come a long way"—omitting the final word, "baby."

At the same time, more women in the academy are complaining that the obstacles to progress seem to be multiplying rather than diminishing. When women are let into these male preserves, the stakes once there are raised. As soon as women were given a piece of the pie, the pie chart exponentially expanded to keep women at a disadvantage.

Nevertheless, momentous transformations have taken place: new and prizewinning scholarship demonstrates the influence of the emerging field of Southern women's history generally and of African American women's history in particular.

The coming of age of Southern women's history, its vibrant ascension during the past half century, has been achieved in no small part through feminist and activist scholarship. In 1985, when Jacqueline Jones published *Labor of Love, Labor of Sorrow: Black Women, Work and the Family from Slavery to the Present*, her accolades demonstrated the quality and distinction of her work and the hunger for this emerging field.[9] Jones's work was a short-listed finalist for the Pulitzer Prize and won the Bancroft Prize, the Philip Taft Labor History Book Award, the Julia Cherry Spruill Book Award from the SAWH, and the Brown Memorial Book Award from the Association of Black Women Historians. Jones exemplifies how scholars in Southern history employ racial and gender dynamics to redefine the field, pursuing emerging paths to create Southern women's histories.

Southern women have always had a past, but the mythic qualities ascribed to them meant that, at times, stereotypes overshadowed real women's lives. Many histories remain one- or two-dimensional, despite today's eagerness for layered, indeed, intersectional stories. The simpering belle and the obstreperous Mammy are being retired by a strong, steady march of new and important monographs that directly challenge such caricatures.

Anne Scott's frontal assault on the Southern belle is captured in the subtitle of her influential 1970 monograph, *The Southern Lady: From Pedestal to Politics (1830–1930)*. After this landmark study through the turn of the next century, the focus on antebellum mistresses monopolized gender studies within Southern history—although the imbalance definitely seems to be correcting in the early decades of the twenty-first century. By the 1980s and 1990s, a virtual cottage industry had devoted itself to reconceptualizing the role of white women within plantation culture.[10] An outpouring of new works exploring diaries and letters, including multigenerational plantation epics, followed. C. Vann Woodward's *Mary Chesnut's Civil War* won the 1982 Pulitzer Prize and stimulated an avalanche of controversy and fresh assessments of Chesnut as well as her white Southern sisters.[11] A sharp, revisionist perspective was introduced in 1990 by Nell Irvin Painter's *The Secret Eye: The Journal of Ella Gertrude Clanton Thomas, 1848–1889*.[12] Thus, subversion studies launched when racial and class nuances were introduced, and scholars began to exploit a wider range of theoretical perspectives on primary material.

The newly visible cohort of Southern black women moved into the foreground of plantation studies. Edited volumes such as Gerda Lerner's *Black Women in White America: A Documentary History* (1972) and Dorothy Sterling's *We Are Your Sisters: Black Women in the Nineteenth Century* (1984) pioneered this transformation.[13]

Robert Manson Myers's *The Children of Pride: A True Story of Georgia and the Civil War* won the National Book Award for History in 1972. This collection of more than twelve hundred annotated letters chronicles the lives of the white slaveholding Jones family of Liberty County, Georgia. Thirty-five years later, Erskine Clarke won the Bancroft Prize for *Dwelling Place: A Plantation Epic* (2007), which offered a surgical striking of the set of this "true story of Georgia." Clarke illuminates the African American presence as more than serving the white protagonists. This fresh perspective chronicles the struggles of the enslaved, integrating black lives into this plantation world. Clarke foregrounds the enslaved Lizzy Jones, and by scouring church records, court documents, and weaving together memories from the black community, he uncovers a "truer" story of Jones. With this reconfiguring of the Southern past, Southern stories became more calibrated and more complete.[14]

Scholars such as Thavolia Glymph, in her formidable *Out of the House of Bondage: The Transformation of the Plantation Household* (2008), presented powerful new narratives that overturned previous historical conventions and launched new lines of inquiry.[15] Kimberly Wallace-Sanders has shown how wealthy white women of the slaveholding class maintained their privilege through farming out the role of "other mothering" to enslaved females, especially those they characterized as "plantation mammies." Stephanie Jones-Rogers won the Lerner-Scott Prize in 2013 for her dissertation, which was the basis for *"They Were Her Property": White Women as Slave Owners in the American South* (2019).

This scholarship has directly challenged previous interpretations of slaveholding women's roles within plantation society. Jones-Rogers's argument highlights white women's direct investment in maintaining the slave economy. Further, by reexamining the WPA narratives, among other sources, she exposed patterns of cruelty and barbarity practiced by mistresses toward the enslaved. These scholarly interventions have refined the field, highlighting intersectionality within Southern studies.[16]

The New South and subsequent eras have been redefined as well by important, transformative work during the past few decades. Glenda Gilmore's prizewinning *Gender and Jim Crow: Women and the Politics of White Supremacy in North Carolina, 1896–1920* (1996) was part of a mighty tide that had tremendous ripple effects, encouraging dozens of scholars to rewrite histories of the decades between the Civil War and the civil rights era.[17] Oral histories have contributed to important, innovative volumes: works such as Susan Tucker's *Telling Memories among Southern Women: Domestic Workers and Their Employers in the Segregated South* and Jacquelyn Dowd Hall, Mary Murphy, et al.'s *Like a Family: The Making of a Southern Cotton Mill World.*[18] Intersecting histories emerge from new methodological braiding, including volumes such as Winifred Breines's *The Trouble Between Us: An Uneasy History of White and Black Women in the Feminist Movement* and Patricia Scott-Bell's *The Firebrand and the First Lady: Portrait of a Friendship; Pauli Murray, Eleanor Roosevelt, and the Struggle for Social Justice.*[19]

Autobiographies from both white and black women have broadened and deepened the histories of Southern women, offering powerful lenses on the past. Classic volumes include Anne Moody's *Coming of Age in Mississippi* (1968), and *Outside the Magic Circle: The Autobiography of Virginia Foster Durr* (1985).[20] Pauli Murray's *Proud Shoes: The Story of An American Family* illuminates the racial and sexual violence that led to silences within both black communities and white communities concerning interracial connections. Murray was extremely forthcoming about secrets of racial identity and interracial liaisons but remained silent on the subject of her own sense of sexual ambiguity. It would take decades and an emboldened biographer to tackle the issues surrounding Murray's sexual identity—as she had even consulted a surgeon about the possibility of being intersexed, of being a man trapped in a woman's body, a completely veiled subject at the time.[21] Equally radicalizing for rereading Southern women's writings are the emerging lesbian voices of the Southern LGBTQIA community, as exemplified within Connie Griffin's pioneering anthology, *Crooked Letter i: Coming Out in the South* (2016).[22]

The high quality and vast quantity of engaging work on the civil rights era is an ongoing challenge for scholars trying to keep up with the field. Naturally, memoir and autobiography play a significant role in rebranding the movement as one in which women and men equally participated, even though the malignant neglect of women's contributions persists in most narrative histories. One of the first SAWH book prizes went to *The Montgomery Bus Boycott and* the *Women Who Started It: The Memoir of Jo Ann Gibson Robinson* in 1988.[23] A landmark study, Sara Evans's *Personal Politics: The Roots of Women's Liberation in the Civil Rights Movement & the New Left* first appeared in 1979 and is in its ninth printing. Only a few years ago, Rosa Parks was the lone female name associated with the civil rights movement, with maybe a nod to Coretta Scott King, who was generally consigned to the role of loyal spouse. These subordinate, marginalized frameworks require reform and have prompted significant scholarly interventions.[24]

In recent narratives of the era, women have been added to the ranks of civil rights leadership or local organizers through a continuous rollout of diversifying scholarship. Overhauling our understanding of the intervention of massive nonviolent protest within the South, of women's vibrant and varied contributions, has been an uphill battle. But the steady flow of renovation has made civil rights scholarship one of the ramparts most heroically mounted during any feminist bombardments. It is difficult to keep up with the contemporary cascade of scalding revisionism, which includes the groundbreaking 2010 study by Danielle McGuire, *At the Dark End of the Street: Black Women, Rape, and Resistance.*[25] Several of these important volumes have won prizes, attracted wider audiences through classroom adoption, or both.

Critically acclaimed essays have stimulated scores of younger scholars to launch innovative investigations in the wake of pioneering conceptual frameworks. Several distinguished articles include Darlene Clark Hine's "Rape and the Inner Lives of Black Women in the Middle West: Preliminary Thoughts on the Culture of Dissemblance" (1989), Elsa Barkley Brown's "Negotiating and Transforming the Public Sphere: African American Political Life in the Transition from Slavery to Freedom" (1994), Theda Perdue's "Columbus Meets Pocahontas in the American South" (1997), Jennifer Morgan's "'Some Could Suckle over Their Shoulder': Male Travelers, Female Bodies, and the Gendering of Racial Ideology, 1500–1770" (1997), and Jacquelyn Dowd Hall's "The Long Civil Rights Movement and the Political Uses of the Past" (2005), to name but a few.[26]

Nearly a dozen SAWH stalwarts gathered in November 2018 to contemplate how far we've come and the directions in which we need to continue. We hope that our essays might become as useful as those recommended above. Perhaps our collective reflections might serve as signposts for those leaping ahead. We cannot predict what will be lost and what gained, as so many things that disappear seem to come round again. And if they do get stuck in the past, we have the tools to dig them out and the camaraderie to enjoy our excavations.

Our band decided to share personal and political insights about Southern women's histories and about our own struggles negotiating topics, careers, and collective enterprises. We solicited reflections on how our field has been transformed by the networks and generations of women who have created a dynamic new scholarly ethic.

The topics were not dictated, but each author was asked to tackle a broad subject within her wheelhouse. We were instructed not to reinvent the wheel, nor to strike out for any new territory until the final group panel. Individual scholars were encouraged to bring personal experiences into the mix, when appropriate. The diverse paths we represent might offer useful, individualized guidance. Reluctance thankfully faded, conflicts were temporarily suspended, and our gathering took on a festive air. Sisterhood indeed sparked an energizing chord.

We recognized that it would be a foolish and strange notion to attempt to sum up a half century of the work in our various fields, so this goal was quickly scratched. With more flexible boundaries and the license to incorporate our own stories, we set our clocks and met at the University of Florida, where for three days we exchanged, debated, and, above all, cherished reflections together. We hope that the results, shared through this volume, will benefit current and future generations.

Catherine Clinton's essay sings the praises of archivists and librarians who most often address our concerns and offer their insight with abundant enthusiasm. The great expansion of Southern women's history over the past half century has been fueled in part by the pioneering archival projects launched by women's historians and other specialists. These specialists have assembled collections and launched guides to resources, both to create pathways into established libraries, archives, and collections and to advance research and writing in the field.

Many of us shared tales about someone who made our research efforts significantly easier. During those frustrating early days, we were told repeatedly, "Sorry, but." But hearing that there are "no sources" for writing about women can turn into teachable moments. With their feet firmly planted, these intrepid researchers did not skulk round the back but faced zealous gatekeepers, firmly ringing the bell and insisting on gaining entry.

By sharing our stories, we remembered how vastly improved both the guides to these collections and our access to the repositories have become. From the "Long Women's Movement in the American South" at the Southern Oral History Program at the University of North Carolina in Chapel Hill to the Collection of Writings by Virginia Women in the Lipscomb Library, Randolph-Macon Woman's College, from the Sallie Bingham Center for Women's

History and Culture at Duke University to the Women Military Aviators Digital Archive at Texas Woman's University, the scope and expanse of Southern women's contributions to the past are being solicited, sorted, and digitized for public consumption.

Clinton solicits and shares archivists' responses to her online queries and incorporates tales of discovery from talented researchers into her essay. The early stages of bringing down the barricades consisted of a cadre of younger scholars questioning the womanless landscape for Southern history and demanding time and attention from an older generation. Pioneering feminists strategized and laid the foundation for building a pulsing network of sister scholars.

Southern women's history has emerged from the shadows and become a significant, central aspect of understanding historical change, particularly in late-twentieth-century social movements. A local community leader like Rosa Parks became a national symbol, one of the true heroes who led America out of the dark ages of segregation, and in later life, emerged as an icon: the first woman to lie in state at the rotunda of the U.S. Capitol.

By applying pressure in a positive and persistent manner, historians and activists pushed ahead and created the framework for Southern women's history to flourish. A flurry of handbooks emerged as librarians and archivists began to amass new materials, to prepare and publish elaborate and engaging guides, and to connect these resources to larger questions in the field. The project of Southern women's history has become less about gatekeeping and more about raising the roof.

Historian and current dean of her college at Wake Forest University, Michele Gillespie is no stranger to contested issues. But she has taken on one of the most controversial historical battlegrounds for feminist scholars: the American Civil War. Over the last three decades, the scholarship of historians of women, gender, and sexuality has transformed our understanding of the Confederacy and the Civil War. With the publication of their 1992 anthology *Divided Houses: Gender and the Civil War* (1992), editors Catherine Clinton and Nina Silber hoped that by exploring gender and women, be they enslaved, working class, or elite, might launch a generational shift in Civil War studies. Gillespie says that this exciting work puts women at the battle scene—as nurses, spies, soldiers, prostitutes, laundresses, and refugees—even as it explores the ways that women on the home front engaged in wars within their own households to maintain their social status and ideological beliefs and keep their menfolk alive.

Scholarship has demonstrated that gendered understandings in the American South were radically altered by the acute crisis of wartime experience and the attendant consequences that reorganized Southern society in the post-emancipation world. Gillespie points to exciting scholarship that insists that Southern women fought hard to construct and claim citizenship. She examines bold new work on African American women that documents their fights for freedom. Gillespie suggests that leaving women out is an unacceptable strategy that can cripple otherwise talented scholars.

Melissa Walker offers a multifaceted appreciation of the value of SAWH's track record. Her piece, "A Place Where Women Can Feel Valued, or Why Academic Professional Associations Matter, Especially for Women," describes the early days and fledgling goals of the SAWH and then pivots to expand on the organization's commitment to professional development. The SAWH specializes in supporting younger scholars in the field, particularly women who work on gender and sexuality. The SHA caucus that became first a committee and then the independent SAWH organization promotes mentorship rather than the more gladiatorial aspects featured within the culture of other groups. Historian Elizabeth Jacoway says, "I think that the fact that [the SAWH] is so wildly successful speaks to the need . . . women . . . feel to have a place where they can go . . . and feel that they are valued."

Through organizational records, oral histories, and current testimony from SAWH members, Walker investigates the evolution of the SAWH's mentoring programs and its dedication to nurturing women's history. She highlights those sisterly networks that characterized the group's dedicated purpose.

From the first annual address, offered by A. Elizabeth Taylor at the 1979 SHA meeting in Atlanta, to the establishment of book and article prizes to honor work on women's history and work by female historians, the organization has increased the visibility of outstanding scholarship by and about women.[27]

Seeking to expand opportunities for historians studying women to present their work, the group in 1988 organized its first triennial Conference on Southern Women's History at Converse College. Nearly four hundred men and women—graduate students and senior scholars—gathered for formal presentations and informal discussions of all things Southern women's history, which gave rise to a series of conferences. The eleventh, and most recent, gathering was held at the University of Alabama in 2018, with the next scholarly program scheduled to be hosted at the University of Kentucky in 2021.

Informal conversations at these meetings highlighted the fact that female historians struggled to find publication opportunities. In response, SAWH leaders decided to collect, edit, and publish the best papers from the conference, and an ongoing Southern Women series was established at the University of Missouri Press (see appendix C).

The SAWH nurtured graduate students by including a graduate representative on its executive council and by offering graduate students deeply discounted membership fees. In addition, many members gift membership to their graduate students, inviting them to meetings to connect postgraduates with peers and to take advantage of the opportunity to meet and mix with senior scholars. The organization also developed a mentoring toolkit, an online collection of advice on topics including selecting a graduate school, navigating the Job Search, grants and fellowships, and minority faculty issues. A research fellowship for mid-career scholars was added. Walker is particularly attuned to these issues, having retired from full-time teaching to coach and advise clients about how to navigate transitions and maintain equilibrium during challenging times.

Walker chronicles how Southern women's history has generally nurtured newcomers, eschewing the "deep end of the pool" techniques to which too many younger scholars are subjected. Any graduate student giving his or her first paper at a SAWH meeting is matched up with a senior scholar for a pre-delivery conference pep talk. Such measures tend to reassure and might even instill confidence—but this mentor match-up is a means to reduce the butterflies that might settle in a young scholar's stomach before public speaking.

Cherisse Jones-Branch's essay, "'Can the Sistas Get Some History, Too?': Transformations in Southern Black Women's History," is full of buoyant optimism, even as she delineates some of the rough patches on the path to tenure, an endowed professorship, and perhaps even joining an international conference circuit. Jones-Branch discusses how her subject, namely, rural black women, has suffered marginalization in African American history, in American women's history, and in Southern history. But she believes this triple burden now places her subject squarely at the core of contemporary issues. She focuses on how black women became leaders during campaigns for civil and educational activism, pushing for community uplift. She discusses Evelyn Brooks Higginbotham's *Righteous Discontent* as a monograph that highlights black women's critical roles in cultivating churches as activist spaces. Jones-Branch urges Southern historians to give rural black women their due, noting that most scholars of African American history focus on the urban environment—even in the South, and, unaccountably, even before the twentieth century. She astutely suggests that scholars must pull their heads out of the "slavery sand trap" and look at black women in *freedom* as much as in bondage. Her early work on home demonstration agents, and on one in particular, Sara Z. Daniels, who lost her job owing to her civil rights activism, has opened up new perspectives on Southern black women's histories. She welcomes the "scaffolding" that a previous generation of scholars has erected to start building a strong framework for understanding the majority experience of black women until the late twentieth century. She makes a case for expanding the race, place, and gender dynamics within the field to provide a firmer foundation for showcasing these emblematic women.

Glenda Gilmore's "Present at the Birth of a New History: A Southern Midwives' Tale" is a rallying cry, calling us to attention; we historians might not be as acutely aware as she is of the opportunities on which we must build. She outlines five major interventions that "rewrote Southern history at large."

Gilmore suggests that these revised narratives need to be nurtured and maintained by the next generation. She heralds those innovative monographs that connected family, personal lives, civic structures, and politics. She further declares that she was a witness to and participant in a unique opportunity to reinterpret and revitalize the overall field of Southern history.

Gilmore makes bold and accessible claims that the local can produce insights of global significance—and we have seen great strides made in the "global South" project of the past few decades. Although Gilmore makes a case for a historiographical thread and a "chain of individual scholars" and institutions that she suggests generated the field. A counter argument could be made that out of one river, several streams thrive. But she offers hope that the informal culture of mentoring might be one way of ensuring that this revolutionary academic field will not backslide. Indeed, the sisterly networks created a climate of progressive improvements.

Gilmore celebrates those Southern historians who collaborated over the past few decades to transform their field while building a community of scholars to follow a new model of academic practice. Because this community had to be built from scratch, most often by women who faced marginalization, it adopted a transformative model of scholarship that is collaborative, supportive, and capacious. By setting aside the hierarchy, exclusion, and adversarial personal attacks that are all too familiar within heady historical circles, scholars of Southern women's history often put their collective mission first. In this way, the greatest generation will always be the next one, as we embrace new ideas and rededicate ourselves to younger scholars on the rise.

At the invitation of the Milbauer Symposium at the University of Florida, we were able to both tackle the hard questions and cheer ourselves on during the bleaker times for historians and scholars seeking to advance the project of the SAWH and like-minded professional associations. We may have embraced a narrow set of reforms during the organizations' early days, but hitting our stride at fifty, members of our group wished to praise and preserve those values that have led us into productive and positive outcomes. At the same time, several of us were tasked with addressing the challenges of the next half century: how can we make sure we are not losing our gains? How can we draw in larger and larger numbers to undertake significant collective tasks with greater urgency? How can we revive the sisterly spirit that underpinned such significant gains?

If our work is to be recognized, can we not set up standards that reject those who would perpetuate single-sex stereotypes? Has a scholar of Southern women's history ever written an article or monograph and not mentioned men? When the reverse is no longer true, will that bring us parity? Cold comfort? Or, more likely, a gigantic backlash? Work on Southern women has roared down the pike in the past half century, establishing outposts all along the way. But this progress brought out the lion tamers, cracking a whip and prancing in high boots and scarlet jacket, trying to keep ferocious felines at bay!

What follows are five interrogatory, reflective, and at times piercing interventionist insights into where we are and where we might be going. Each scholar makes her points before moving on to appreciate the next set of competing demands. Our two days of presentations were followed by a final third day whereby we embarked on a freewheeling panel discussion, a roundtable to complete our convening. We roamed widely—with lots of hopes, dreams, plots, and perhaps even a little prayer to launch us into our next fifty years. Although we could not take time to slow down, we did manage to imagine the fun of fireworks, revisions, and sisterly networks in the years ahead.

Acknowledgments

It took more than a village, more than any one department or city or campus to build this network of committed activist scholars scattered across the globe. Southern women's history has been enormously lucky to have the talents of SAWH founders, officers, boards, members, and ongoing supporting organizations for the past fifty years. Through the grace of ongoing hard work toward collective goals and projects, wise and wonderful leadership, and the good fortune we have had to live in interesting, historically challenging times, perhaps our next fifty years will lead us onward to an even more celebratory and memorable centennial in 2070!

This volume is a tribute to many, but particularly to the scholars who gave so generously of their time and talents to contribute essays: Glenda Gilmore, Melissa Walker, Cherisse Jones-Branch, and in particular, Michele Gillespie, who has always been such a strong ally. In addition, I wish to thank those who came to Gainesville and joined with sister scholars to participate in our symposium roundtable on November 29, 2018: Lisa Tendrich Frank, Pippa Holloway, Elizabeth Jacoway, Lauren Pearlman, and Constance Schulz.

Much appreciation to both William A. Link, the Milbauer Professor of History at the University of Florida, and his Frontiers of the American South series for making this publication possible. He was with us every step of the way and we salute his generosity and stewardship. With special thanks to Sian Hunter, of the University Press of Florida, and her team, who assisted in bringing this dream volume to fruition.

Notes

1. Judith N. McArthur, "A. Elizabeth Taylor: Searching for Southern Suffragists," in *Reading Southern History: Essays on Interpreters and Interpretations*, ed. Glen Feldman (Tuscaloosa: University of Alabama Press, 2001), 167. And this generation of pioneers was discouraged from thinking of themselves as viable candidates to become historians, much less that women might be the topic for professional historians. Neither Taylor nor Massey selected subjects relating to women for their dissertations. As Noralee Frankel observes concerning an investigation of gender issues within the AHA: "The [Rose] report did not mince words about the discrimination that women historians faced. It cited a study that stated that those who 'discriminated against women in academic employment also hold general views concerning female inferiority. . . . While addressing women's career concerns, the Rose Report *did not mention women's history as a field of study*" (emphasis added). See Noralee Frankel, "Remembering the Rose Report," *Perspectives on History* (November 2010): https://www.historians.org/publications-and-directories/perspectives-on-history/november-2010/remembering-the-rose-report.

2. See Melissa Walker, "A Place Where Women Can Feel Valued, or Why Academic Professional Associations Matter, Especially for Women," chapter 3.

3. Catherine Clinton and Michele Gillespie, eds., *Taking Off the White Gloves: Southern Women and Women Historians* (Columbia: University of Missouri Press, 1998).

4. The evidence indicates a tectonic shift within the last twenty years, with *five* women at the helm of the AHA *in a row*: Linda K. Kerber (2006), Barbara Weinstein (2007), Gabrielle M. Spiegel (2008), Laurel Thatcher Ulrich (2009), and Barbara Metcalf (2010).

5. Interview with Anne Scott, Constance Schulz, and Elizabeth Turner, eds., *Clio's Southern Sisters* (Columbia: University of Missouri Press, 2004), 38.

6. See American Historical Association, "The Rose Report," (1970) appendix E: Proportion of Women to Men Receiving PhD and MA Degrees between 1900 and 1970. Accessed March 31, 2019: https://www.historians.org/about-aha-and-membership/aha-history-and-archives/historical-archives/report-of-the-aha-committee-on-the-status-of-women/appendix-e-proportion-of-women-to-men-receiving-phd-and-ma-degrees-between-1900-and-1970.

7. Interview with A. Elizabeth Taylor, Constance Schulz, and Elizabeth Turner, eds., *Clio's Southern Sisters* (Columbia: University of Missouri Press, 2004), 26.

8. See Glenda Gilmore, "Present at the Birth of a New History: A Southern Midwives' Tale," chapter 5.

9. Jacquelyn Dowd Hall, *Revolt Against Chivalry: Jessie Daniel Ames and the Women's Campaign Against Lynching* (New York: Columbia University Press, 1979), and Jacqueline Jones, *Labor of Love, Labor of Sorrow: Black Women, Work and the Family from Slavery to the Present* (New York: Basic, 1985). Both of these books have stimulated revised editions: Hall in 1993, and Jones in 1990.

10. See Catherine Clinton, *The Plantation Mistress: Woman's World in the Old South* (New York: Pantheon, 1982); Elizabeth Fox-Genovese, *Within the Plantation Household: Black and White Women of the Old South* (Chapel Hill: University of North Carolina, 1988); Marli Weiner, *Mistresses and Slaves: Plantation Women in South Carolina, 1830–80* (Urbana: University of Illinois Press, 1998). Drew Gilpin Faust's *Mothers of Invention: Women of the Slaveholding South in the American Civil War* (Chapel Hill: University of North Carolina, 1996) challenged many previous Civil War scholars to reassess their dismissal of female influence on secession and their roles in Confederate nationalism. See also Michael O'Brien, ed., *An Evening When Alone: Four Journals of Single Women in the South, 1827–67* (Charlottesville: University Press of Virginia, 1993), and Laura F. Edwards, *Scarlett Doesn't Live Here Any More: Southern Women in the Civil War Era* (Urbana: University of Illinois Press, 2000).

11. See in particular Thavolia Glymph, "African-American Women in the Literary Imagination of Mary Boykin Chesnut," in *Slavery, Secession, and Southern History*, ed. Robert Louis Paquette and Louis A. Ferleger (Charlottesville: University Press of Virginia, 2000), 140–56. See also Elisabeth Muhlenfeld, "Mary Boykin Chesnut: Civil War Redux," in *South Carolina Women: Their Lives and Times*, ed. Marjorie Julian Spruill et al., 1:249–51 (Athens: University of Georgia Press, 2009).

12. Nell Irvin Painter, ed., *The Secret Eye: The Journal of Ella Gertrude Clanton Thomas, 1848–1889* (Chapel Hill: University of North Carolina Press, 1990).

13. Gerda Lerner, *Black Women in White America: A Documentary History* (New York: Pantheon, 1972), and Dorothy Sterling, *We Are Your Sisters: Black Women in the Nineteenth Century* (New York: W. W. Norton: 1984).

14. In some ways, the concept of "Southern women" has been enlarged by revisiting women to discuss how their Southern birth/upbringing or how their escapes from the South illuminate Southern womanhood. See, for example, Catherine Clinton, *Harriet Tubman: The Road to Freedom* (Boston: Little Brown, 2004); Mark Perry, *Lift Up Thy Voice: The Sarah and Angelina Grimke's Family Journey from Slaveholders to Civil Rights Leaders* (New York: Viking, 2001).

15. Thavolia Glymph, *Out of the House of Bondage: The Transformation of the Plantation Household* (New York: Cambridge University Press, 2008).

16. Kimberly Wallace-Sanders, *Mammy: A Century of Race, Gender, and Southern Memory* (Ann Arbor: University of Michigan Press, 2008); and Stephanie Jones-Rogers, *They Were Her Property: White Women as Slaveowners in the American South* (New Haven: Yale University Press, 2019).

17. Glenda Gilmore, *Gender and Jim Crow: Women and the Politics of White Supremacy in North Carolina, 1896–1920* (Chapel Hill: University of North Carolina, 1996). See also Linda Reed, *Simple Decency and Common Sense: The Southern Conference Movement, 1983–1963* (Bloomington: Indiana University Press, 1991); Evelyn Brooks-Higginbotham, *Righteous Discontent: The Women's Movement in the Black Baptist Church, 1880–1920* (Cambridge, Mass.: Harvard University Press, 1993); Tera W. Hunter, *To 'Joy My Freedom: Southern Black Women's Lives and Labors after the Civil War* (Cambridge, Mass.: Harvard University Press,

1997); Rosalyn Terborg-Penn, *African American Women in the Struggle for the Vote, 1850–1920* (Bloomington: Indiana University Press, 1998); Tiffany M. Gill, *Beauty Shop Politics: African American Women's Activism in the Beauty Industry* (Urbana: University of Illinois Press, 2010); Sharon D. Kennedy-Nolle, *Writing Reconstruction: Race, Gender and Citizenship in the Postwar South* (Chapel Hill: University of North Carolina, 2015); Talitha LeFlouria, *Chained in Silence: Black Women and Convict Labor in the New South* (Chapel Hill: University of North Carolina, 2015); Robyn Spencer, *The Revolution Has Come: Black Power, Gender and the Black Panther Party in Oakland* (Durham, N.C.: Duke University Press, 2016); Treva Lindsey, *Colored No More: Reinventing Black Womanhood in Washington, D.C.* (Urbana: University of Illinois Press, 2017); and Brittney C.Cooper, *Beyond Respectability: The Intellectual Thought of Race Women* (Urbana: University of Illinois Press, 2017).

18. Susan Tucker, *Telling Memories among Southern Women: Domestic Workers and Their Employers in the Segregated South* (Baton Rouge: Louisiana State University Press, 1988); and Jacquelyn Dowd Hall, Mary Murphy, et al., *Like a Family: The Making of a Southern Cotton Mill World* (Chapel Hill: University of North Carolina, 1987).

19. Winifred Breines, *The Trouble between Us: An Uneasy History of White and Black Women in the Feminist Movement* (New York: Oxford University Press, 2006); and Patricia Bell-Scott, *The Firebrand and the First Lady: Portrait of a Friendship: Pauli Murray, Eleanor Roosevelt, and the Struggle for Social Justice* (New York: Knopf, 2016).

20. Virginia Foster Durr, *Outside the Magic Circle: The Autobiography of Virginia Foster Durr*, ed. Barnard Hollinger (Tuscaloosa: University of Alabama Press, 1985).

21. See Rosalind Rosenberg, *Jane Crow: the Life of Pauli Murray* (New York: Oxford University Press, 2017). See also Kathryn Schulz, "The Many Lives of Pauli Murray," *New Yorker*, April 10, 2017.

22. Connie Griffin, ed., *Crooked Letter i: Coming Out in the South* (Montgomery, Ala.: New South, 2016).

23. Jo Ann Gibson, *The Montgomery Bus Boycott and the Women Who Started It: The Memoir of Jo Ann Gibson Robinson* (Knoxville: University of Tennessee Press, 1987). This book appeared with a foreword by David Garrow, which unfortunately resulted in the organization mistakenly preparing only one plaque for the prize—which was presented to David Garrow, as the book's "editor." During this error, Jo Ann Gibson Robinson was relegated to a separate, and many felt unequal, status when the book was in fact almost entirely her own autobiographical writing. The SAWH was engulfed in a crisis with this first foray into awarding scholarly prizes—and recovered only after many apologies, mea culpa, and a new plaque. See correspondence on deposit at the SAWH Papers held at the Special Collections at Wilson Library, UNC Chapel Hill. The irony of giving a white man the public recognition for a volume that was the voice of a black woman contributor to the Montgomery Bus Boycott was not lost on critics who felt it reflected a bias within the organization and within the larger profession generally. Since the mid-1980s, the SAWH has struggled to improve its reputation and to acknowledge and erode the white privilege that the field of Southern women's studies has too often cultivated. This continues to be a preoccupation of the membership and certainly of its past and current leadership.

24. Often, these corrective perspectives are introduced by those women participants themselves, for example, Constance Curry's *Deep in Our Hearts: Nine White Women in the Freedom Movement* (Athens: University of Georgia Press, 2000).

25. Danielle L. McGuire, *At the Dark End of the Street: Black Women, Rape and Resistance* (New York: Knopf, 2010). See also Chana Kai Lee, *For Freedom's Sake: The Life of Fannie Lou Hamer* (Urbana: University of Illinois Press, 1999); Lynne Olson, *Freedom's Daughters: The Unsung Heroines of the Civil Rights Movement from 1830–1970* (New York: Scribner's, 2001); Barbara Ransby, *Ella Baker and the Black Freedom Movement: A Radical Democratic Vision* (Chapel Hill: University of North Carolina Press, 2003); Kimberly Springer, *Living for the Revolution: Black Feminist Organizations, 1968–1980* (Durham, N.C.: Duke University Press, 2005); Davis W. Houck and David E. Dixon, eds., *Women and the Civil Rights Movement, 1954–65* (Jackson: University Press of Mississippi, 2009); Ashley Farmer, *Remaking Black Power: How Black Women Transformed an Era* (Chapel Hill: University of North Carolina, 2017).

26. Darlene Clark Hine, "Rape and the Inner Lives of Black Women in the Middle West: Preliminary thoughts on the Culture of Dissemblance," *Signs* 4, no. 4 (1989) 912–21; Elsa Barkley Brown's "Negotiating and Transforming the Public Sphere: African American Political Life in the Transition from Slavery to Freedom," *Public Culture* 7, no. 1 (Fall 1994): 107–46; Theda Perdue, "Columbus Meets Pocahontas in the American South," *Southern Cultures* 3, no. 1 (Spring 1997), 4–21; Jennifer Morgan, "'Some Could Suckle Over Their Shoulder': Male Travelers, Female Bodies, and the Gendering of Racial Ideology, 1500–1770," *William and Mary Quarterly* 54, 3rd series (January 1997): 167–92; and Jacquelyn Dowd Hall, "The Long Civil Rights Movement and the Political Uses of the Past," *Journal of American History* 91, no. 4 (March 2005), 1233–63.

27. The SAWH suffered a slight public relations problem with the establishment of the Willie Lee Rose Prize, which was to be given to the *woman* who writes the best book in Southern history. This restriction stirred up controversy and was opposed by some women, but particularly male supporters of the organization, such as feminist scholar Carl Degler, who publicly objected to this sexually segregated prize. SAWH correspondence files, Special Collections, Wilson Library, Chapel Hill, UNC. Many members have discussed the possibility of trying to shift the specifications for the prize (terms that were not dictated by a donor), as many SAWH members regularly collect prizes from the SHA, SHEAR, and other organizations, so the reluctance to have women serve on prize juries and win awards seems to have eroded over the years.

1

Barbarians at the Doorbell

Tales from the Archives

CATHERINE CLINTON

In the 1970s, archivists throughout the South felt the pressure from invading hordes of researchers, many of them hell-bent on breaking down the barriers that kept women's issues, women's lives, and women's records buried in a past that undervalued female experience. If women's papers were interpolated in historical collections, then they might not even be catalogued in detail, instead lying dormant in file boxes. A new generation of librarians and archivists forged alliances and created initiatives that would change American history, with an outpouring of guides and bibliographies.[1]

Female scholars were becoming increasingly adamant that they would mine the buried riches—with or without permission. They would storm the bastions of Southern history and change the narrative. Multiple voices began to ripple across the historical landscape, calling for changes. These protests might have been disruptive, but these were barbarians who used the doorbells—ringing persistently and loudly to announce their arrival and being unwilling to take the litany of "nos" for their answer.

During my first year of graduate school back in 1975, I decided to visit an archive during the fall break so that I could research some primary material. I was working on an abolitionist woman, Maria Weston Chapman, and was thinking she might be good material for a biography.[2] I trekked north from Princeton to Boston. Nearly forty-five years later, I am glad my plan got derailed by my encounters with a chilly manuscript librarian and a manuscript access policy that left me cold. I spent three days cooling my heels, waiting for a special delivery letter from James McPherson, my graduate advisor (who claimed my research was preliminary work on my dissertation) so that I could be granted access to women's abolitionist society papers held in special collections at the Boston Public Library.

Without this letter, gatekeepers denied me entrance: the doors were closed. When I did gain entrance, I was still greeted with suspicion: my requests for collections appeared to be an irritation, if not an imposition. The print guides gave little indication of material on women, and even less on women of color. After I finally got my hands on a file folder of documents, a desk attendant would carefully search *each* folder to make sure all pages were returned—even though I had sat no more than a few feet away and she had watched my every move as I examined these papers. I experienced the slow *drip-drip-drip* of bureaucratic delay as I fetched new folders and returned perused ones.

Besides setting my teeth on edge, this roadblock taught me valuable lessons: always call ahead and try to get the name of a person who might be knowledgeable and/or helpful. Despite the technological developments of the past half century, *calling* and finding a contact continues to be solid advice. I emphasize phone contact to current students who are overly fond of the internet. Email might appear equally time-saving, but a conversation can pave the way to not only getting answers to what you want to know but also obtaining information you didn't even know you needed.

I sensed during my first semester of graduate school that Southern history might prove compelling. I had already been on a wild ride: earning a master's abroad, in the United Kingdom, then following a detour, teaching in North Africa, before settling down in Princeton for my doctorate. I warmed to the intensity of Southern history. Southern sources would lure me away from New England or mid-Atlantic affinities: Southward Ho!

Shortly after my encounter at the Boston Public Library, I attended my first Southern Historical Association (in Washington, D.C.) and met up with women who had recently organized the Southern Association of Women Historians (SAWH, later renamed the Southern Association *for* Women Historians).[3] This propelled me on a winding path that has led to my current commitment to celebrating the past half century of exploring Southern women's stories and working within the SAWH.

American women's history was just taking off then, and many of us were eager to catch the wave, to be swept up in the growing crusade to create a new social history—a history that includes women and men, black and white, native and immigrant—a holistic approach that included a renewed focus on the underrepresented, the unlettered, the lost but not forgotten. Disruptions in the flow of ideas and books about great white men and their big doings were glacially slow.

Female protestors, hoping to change the historical curricular landscape, launched assaults on patriarchy and the politics of exclusion. Female professors began to stoke the imaginations of legions of students, eager to recognize women's voices within and contributions to the past. In the early 1980s, the textbook market caught on, and Mary Beth Norton was the first female lead author on a major American history textbook. The effect of women's history was just beginning to be felt in department after department, classroom after classroom, campus after campus. Over forty years later, *A People and a Nation*, by Norton et al. (with three other women on the masthead), is in its eleventh printing, and in 2019, Norton is the 133rd president of the American Historical Association.[4]

My colleagues will be chronicling some of the transformative changes within key fields of Southern history, surveying some historiographical developments and significant organizational renovations. I want to share my thoughts about those people and places that have made so much of our work possible over the past five decades: libraries, archives, and those who have helped to transform Southern women's histories.

I want to pay tribute to the unsung agents of change who have made a difference and to highlight the grinding work that goes on behind the scenes. The stories of scholars who championed the cause of women's histories, who demanded access and accountability, remain unchronicled. The strike force dedicated themselves to reshaping accessibility within the archives; scholars began multiple campaigns—a steady barrage of suggestions and demands—to create a larger, more diverse body of materials available to archival sleuths. This web of Southern scholarly investigations created a network of collegiality and sisterhood that fueled several generations of doctoral students, which energized a field in which a hundred flowers bloomed.

Following this transformation, state archives would no longer list material on women as "not of political interest"—the heading under which I had first found collections of materials that included valuable records that assisted me in excavating the voices of early-nineteenth-century plantation mistresses. This research became the basis of both my dissertation and my first book. In the earliest days of the feminist resurgence, I met up with so many colleagues on the research trail, all with similar tales to tell. Sandy Treadway (former SAWH president and current librarian of the State of Virginia) recalled for me an example of scholarly activism:

> In 1991, when I was working as an editor and historian in the Publications Department at the Library of Virginia, I received a call from the archives research room telling me that a graduate student from Yale University

was doing research at the Library and was wondering if she could talk with me. She was hoping to write a dissertation on women in public and political life in antebellum Virginia but was having trouble finding source material. In describing her research topic, the archivists she spoke with explained to her that since women could not vote in the nineteenth century, we would not have anything in our collection that documented what she was looking for. Our archivists thought about politics and political expression in very traditional ways—in terms of voting and office holding—and they were correct that women could not do that in the nineteenth century. But this student knew that antebellum Virginia women did care about the important issues of their day and her instincts were correct—she just needed to figure out where to find the evidence. In the course of my own research, I had come across a tantalizing article in a Richmond newspaper from the 1840s about Lucy Johnson Barbour, widow of one of Virginia's governors, who was trying to enlist women in a fund-raising effort to commission a statue to Henry Clay, longtime standard bearer for the Whig Party, and place it in Virginia's Capitol Square. I was certain there was an important story there and suggested that she find out more. I also suggested the Library's collection of petitions sent to the General Assembly by citizens seeking assistance or redress that only the legislature could provide. I had seen many from women among the hundreds of petitions filed in the antebellum period and suspected that these might serve as windows into women's thoughts and activities in the public sphere. The student in question was Elizabeth Varon, now a distinguished chair professor of history at the University of Virginia.[5]

Sandy goes on to explain that not only do archivists assist researchers but scholars enable archivists to reframe their ideas and assist in making collections more transparent to a wider range of investigators. The push-pull effect of the 1970s and 1980s created an awareness that more needed to be done to reframe archival resources.

This give-and-take remains transformative. But now, clearly the archivists have taken the lead. Several generations of researchers have been given a comfortable berth, a seat at the table—thanks to the spirited engagement of Southern archivists, librarians, and curatorial staff across the South.

Not all places seem to have caught up, though, and a few might even be drifting backward—for years I relied on Wylma Waites to assist me in finding just about anything I could imagine in the South Carolina Department of Archives and History. She has retired, and when I inquired about any manuscript or archival guide to South Carolina women in their holdings, a recent staffer wrote: "Thank you for your interest in South Carolina history. Our agency collects the permanently valuable colonial, state, county and municipal government records for South Carolina 1671 to ca. 2010. I checked our hardcopy finding aids but could not locate any guide to women's records in our collection. Best wishes on all your research projects."[6] Such a cursory response seems remarkably out of step.

I cannot begin to mention all those who have made such crucial differences in our research lives, but I hope to track some contributions that made a difference during these crucial decades when we began to speed the plow and forge new pathways into the past. Frances Pollard was a welcoming presence for waves of researchers at the Virginia Historical Society, and she rescued many of us from mistakes and connected many of us on our quests. She was a dynamic and important friend to generations of SAWH members who were passing through Richmond.

As former SAWH president and current head of the Library of Virginia, Sandy Treadway, has suggested: "Historians rely on and owe a great debt to archivists and librarians, who identify, acquire and preserve the documents they need to understand and interpret the past. But archivists also rely on the work of historians to help them anticipate the questions and topics that researchers may be interested in, which informs how collections are organized and described so that they meet researchers' needs. The questions that researchers ask also help archivists to see their collections in a new light."[7]

It might seem alphabetical to begin with Alabama, but I think not. There have been women—white gloved and not—who pioneered historical archives in this state. Alabama was one of the first places within the United States, second only to Wisconsin, to collect and organize archival material on *Southern* history. (How many women were behind this effort, we likely will never know.) It was also perhaps one of the first southern archives to drop the color line, as John Hope Franklin recalled being admitted for research without incident.[8]

But I do recall when I arrived on their doorstep in the late 1970s that the Alabama archivists were very apologetic that they did not have any guides to women available, but they nonetheless were excellent stewards of the material. Of course, revisiting Montgomery in the second decade of the twenty-first century, the former Confederate capital now supports the Equal Justice Initiative's Legacy Museum and National Memorial for Peace and Justice—one of the most heralded commemorations established in the modern era: "America's first major effort to confront the vast scope of the racial-terror lynchings that ravaged the African-American community in the South."[9] So it has been a long journey from Confederate bastion to anti-racist commemoration capital.

When my assistant wrote to the Alabama State Archives to ask about their guide to women within their collection, an archivist wrote back: "I'm not sure what kind of list Catherine Clinton was given when she first visited the department, but my guess is that she contacted us beforehand and we compiled a list specifically for her. If so, it might be in the director's papers, but that would be a stretch."[10] However, after my request made the rounds, I was sent a guide that had been compiled in the 1990s—perhaps in response to my initial request. This remains an invaluable resource: a snapshot with an annotated list of more than 150 collections—"Women's History Research Sources: Private Records." This report is now buried within the organization, but it represents the heroic efforts of archivists who responded to the needs of scholars seeking buried treasure within Southern archives. And without this highlighting, how would novice scholars discover the important lives that lay within the five cubic feet on Inez Jesse Turner Baskin, "a reporter with the Negro section of the *Montgomery Advertiser*, as well as a social worker and teacher. Her papers document her life as an African American woman in Montgomery, Ala. before, during, and after the years of the Civil Rights movement." Or who would explore the four cubic feet on Lela Legare, a pioneering pharmacist and graduate of Auburn? The Alabama State Archives also offers Mary D. Waring's Civil War diary, as well as Civil War diarist Kate Cumming and Confederate memorialist Sophia Bibb. This guide highlights women within the civil rights movement and women's suffrage, as well as female participation in education, writer's groups, sororities, and many other key aspects of Southern women's experience.

The 1980s was a time of renovation and awakening, not least because the University of Arkansas Special Collections created a handbook: *Manuscript Resources for Women's Studies*. An NEH grant supported this effort to create a guide in 1989, which was completed under the supervision of the head of research services, Andrea Cantrell. Dr. Cantrell retired in 2010, but her guide lives on, updated and online, hosted by the University of Arkansas Libraries Special Collections.[11] This invaluable resource highlights the more than seven linear feet of Daisy Bates's papers, the more than fifty linear feet collected in the Folklife Collection assembled under the direction of pioneering collector Mary Celestia Parler Randolph (1904–1981), and the trial records of Sara Jane Smith, who was accused of sabotage against the Union during the Civil War. Although convicted and sentenced to be hanged, her execution was delayed and she was released after the war. All of these fascinating women and their work has been not just preserved but showcased in this guide.

Further, Danyelle McNeill put together the guide to women's resources at the Arkansas State Archives and created an online version in 2015 for women's history month.[12] *The Guide to Resources on Women at Howard University* was created by Katharine Salzman in 1998. This annotated guide includes resources available on prominent African American women authors, such as Mary Ann Shadd Cary (nineteenth-century abolitionist and editor), Anna Julia Cooper (turn of the twentieth century memoirist and educator), Angelina Weld Grimke (Harlem Renaissance poet and playwright), Georgia Douglas Johnson (poet and host of a twentieth-century Washington, D.C., literary salon) and Pauli Murray (twentieth-century legal crusader and civil rights activist). This pioneering resource, assembled from the Manuscript Division of the Moorland-Spingarn Research Center, highlights the papers of Lucy Diggs Slowe, an educator and civic leader and the first dean of women at Howard University, as well as women musicians, labor activists, socialists, and other unsung heroines.

I found myself mesmerized by magnanimous treatment from the staff at the Southern Historical Collection (SHC) at the University of North Carolina at Chapel Hill—definitely the mother lode for Southern antebellum studies. I remember describing my topic to the archivists who individually and collectively not only guided me to their favorite collections but also described which sections might be most fruitful for my research. Having such generous, knowledgeable experts offering me this personalized insight lightened my burden and gave me great confidence about my topic. A 1984 guide to the collections included detailed highlights of holdings on Southern women.

The dedicated Southern Historical Collection staff worked closely with a faculty working group in Southern studies, who created a "Southern Research Report" in 1991. As the report described:

> The June 1991 meeting of the Southern Association of Women Historians at the University of North Carolina at Chapel Hill seemed to UNC-CH's Faculty Working Group in Southern Studies and area librarians too good an opportunity to pass up. Given our purposes to foster researches on the South and in our holdings as well as interdisciplinary communication, we seized the occasion. This issue of the working group's Southern Research Report is the result.

As Tim West of the UNC Special Collections describes, the fascinating materials at this legendary archive were enhanced by director Carolyn Wallace's cultivation and showcasing of women's materials. In his article "The Vast and Rich Resources for Women's Studies in the Southern Historical Collection," West details the superb opportunities for researchers, not only of materials in women's collections but also of the papers by women in other collections, for example, material from Flannery O'Connor and Caroline Gordon in the Walker Percy Collection.[13] As Hannah Joyner describes in her wonderful contribution,

> In the spring of 1990, a group of seven graduate students in history at the University of North Carolina at Chapel Hill undertook the creation of a finding aid called "Women's Voices in the Southern Oral History Program (SOHP)." Emily Bingham, Hannah Joyner, Maria Miller, Anne Mitchell, Laura Moore, Cynthia Scherer, and Annette Tappe started the project for a course in Southern women's history taught by Southern Oral History Program Director Jacquelyn Dowd Hall.[14]

Equally enhancing, the UNC website "Documenting the American South" includes the 148 women interviewed in the Southern Oral History Program.[15] These amazing interviews (many transcribed and available) are a vast and invaluable resource. I found it critical to my article on Modjeska Monteith Simkins for *Notable American Women*, as do so many of us working on these significant and, until recently, understudied activists.

In 1977, the North Carolina State Archives created a *Guide to Women's Records*, which (regrettably) is no longer in print. Catherine E. Thompson's historic contribution has been replaced by a plethora of online guides. In nearby Duke University Archives, the first women's history archivist, Ginny Daley, helped create a resource, nicknamed "The Sampler," that has grown into a seriously impressive online guide.[16] This indexed resource offers guides to women's studies, women and education, sexuality studies, and LGBT studies. The current director at Duke University's renowned Bingham Center, Laura Micham, worked with Daley on guides when she was a graduate student. So the expanding and generational work of enhancing the archival access to Southern women's history continues.

Virginia remains an important state for Southern women's resources, with several private as well as state resources. I remember being so cosseted during my time visiting the archives at William and Mary University Libraries in Williamsburg, Virginia. Margaret C. Cook, curator of the Manuscripts and Rare Books at Special Collections, was a terrific cheerleader for the field. She kindly assisted me in obtaining permission to publish extracts from personal letters and gave me wise counsel in so many ways. Cook created a guide to women for her archive, completed in 1983. She is still working as a volunteer for Special Collections.

Virginia became a dynamic growth region for identifying and organizing women's history resources. The James Branch Cabell Library's Special Collections and Archives at Virginia Commonwealth University Libraries created a guide for locating women's papers (completed by Daniel Yanchisin) in the 1980s.

The Library of Virginia reported that when they "had a higher budget and more staff, Jennifer McDaid (who no longer works here) created a research note and two guides regarding resources on women. She first wrote them in 2000 and revised them in 2002."[17] The Virginia Historical Society (VHS) proved enterprising when an NEH grant allowed Gail S. Terry to work on "materials relating to women, African Americans and those whose activities and ancestry did not support the 'Great White Men' focus of Southern history."[18] This work resulted in *Documenting Women's Lives: A User's Guide to Manuscripts at the Virginia Historical Society*.[19] Shortly after this, the VHS moved to an online guide, which is updated regularly with new holdings. At the University of Virginia, a staffer, Robin Wear, compiled a guide while working her desk time in public services. She is no longer with Special Collections, and the guide is available through a third party: Virginia Heritage website.[20] An earlier (anonymous) guide was published in 1993 but includes only a small portion of the manuscript collections— "up to number MSS 3675 when we are now cataloging in MSS 16000s," as a current staffer reports.

Louisiana State University maintains an online subject guide.[21] Florida created a paper guide in 1996 but then advanced to an online resource at the Florida Memory website titled *Guide to Women's History Collections*.

All these amazing guides to resources lured scholars into the archives, and archivists in turn urged researchers to seek and exploit these newly accessible and vibrant materials. These efforts encouraged astonishing new narratives, a new appreciation of understudied lives, burgeoning databases, and a collective resurgence. In no area has there been as much exciting and revisionary work as in the field of African American women's history.[22]

Southern women have moved into the foreground of the civil rights movement through important new oral histories and scholarly excavations. Jo Ann Gibson Robinson's memoir, *The Montgomery Bus Boycott and the Women Who Started It* (1987), won the first SAWH book prize (awarded in 1989), recognizing that the voices of black Southern women needed to be reintroduced into our historical narrative. And even more revolutionary, scholars of African American Southern women's history determined a way to speak for those enslaved women who were given no opportunity to leave ego documents. The creative and empowering recovery of these dormant lives has been a marvelous, energetic campaign.

Jim Downs's work on emancipated women has been featured in the *New York Times*, as his first monograph, *Sick From Freedom: African-American Illness and Suffering during the Civil War and Reconstruction* (2012), highlighted the intersection of gender and race. In an essay drawing on his research, Downs limned a compelling image: "He found her lying in a ditch a few miles away from a Union camp in Augusta, Georgia. The war had been over for almost a year, yet she lay there in the dirt under the hot August sun as if she were a recent casualty from battle. By the end of war, she certainly was free, but the slow and often unorganized reconstruction of the South did not offer her a clear road to freedom. Instead as the Bureau agent who discovered her explained, she had been going 'from pillar to post and had fallen on her knees.'"[23] Downs challenges readers to chart the forces that pushed and pulled women during this tumultuous era. Scores of anonymous black women found themselves in similar straits in post-emancipation America, as female bodies littered the Reconstruction landscape. A phalanx of crusading scholars scour archives so that Southern women will be rescued from obscurity, from anonymity, and woven into contemporary historical narratives.

While researching in Philadelphia, Erica Armstrong Dunbar was reading through eighteenth-century newspapers when she came across the following notice: "Absconded from the household of the President of the United States on Saturday afternoon, ONEY JUDGE, a light Mulatto girl, much freckled, with very black eyes, and bushy black hair—She is of middle stature but slender and delicately made, about 20 years of age."[24] Dunbar was taken aback, pondering, "was George Washington really advertising for a runaway slave in Philadelphia? Who was this Oney Judge? What happened to her? Was she ever captured?"[25] She was even more concerned that Judge was a figure about whom she knew *nothing*. Dunbar devoted nearly a decade to researching this extraordinary character, a former enslaved woman who was able to "defy the most powerful couple in the nation—George and Martha Washington."[26] Dunbar's compelling storytelling brought Judge back from the brink of obscurity into a title role. Her prizewinning *Never Caught: The Washingtons' Relentless Pursuit of Their Runaway Slave, Ona Judge* (2018) not only showcases a remarkable African American who liberated herself and evaded recapture but also sets the stage for appreciating the varieties of experience for black women in the new nation.

Daina Ramey Berry also researched her prizewinning book, *The Price for Their Pound of Flesh: The Value of the Enslaved, from Womb to Grave, in the Building of a Nation* (2018), in Philadelphia. Berry saw a physician's notation at a medical library: "1 Splendid silver wired Human skeleton, a Negro aged 40 years."[27] Berry admitted that the "age of the wired 'subject' gave me pause," but she was even more abashed by the next note: "when living [he] stood 6 feet 4 inches high, [with a] round chest."[28] She realized that the physician probably knew the man before he died and confesses, "I had to sit with that for a few days in order to think about what I wanted to say about it in my book."[29] Her meditations led to an amazing project that engaged scholarship on capitalism and slavery in a way that centers the experience and thinking of the enslaved.

Berry scoured thousands of records to uncover how the price of enslaved people varied by age and gender. Studies of slavery and capitalism have dominated the field of U.S. history, but until the publication of Berry's exhaustive study, no scholar had systematically examined how gender shaped this interaction. Her documentation concerning monetization of the flesh (from birth on through auctions and sales, to the trade in cadavers) shines the spotlight on "price" and its multiple meanings.

Enslaved women have been of particular interest to Southern archivists over the past fifty years. After completing her recent prizewinning study of life on the Canadian border, *Dawn of Detroit: A Chronicle of Slavery and Freedom in the City of the Straits*, Tiya Miles turned southward (once again). At Special Collections at the Addlestone Library at the College of Charleston, managing director of research Mary Jo Fairchild gave Miles access to the materials donated from the Old Slave Mart Museum. As she plowed through the mountains of boxes, she sorted through bills of sale (for enslaved people), advertisements and posters, framed photos and vintage postcards. She encountered some fragile treasures: a plantation recipe book from the 1860s and a blond-white lock of Sarah Grimke's hair (sent by Angelina to a relative in Charleston following Sarah's death). Miles, inspired by these items, suggests, "The museum's materials are just as valuable, perhaps more valuable, for what they illuminate about African American museums and the visionaries who founded and funded them, as for what they said about slave trading in Charleston. I hope more researchers will employ this collection."[30]

Talitha LeFlouria reflects that she had just finished her initial year of graduate school when she paid her first visit to the Georgia Archives. She had some trepidation, because she had heard archival horror stories about black female scholars who had been disrespected and denied access and even had given up before they got started. This was not LeFlouria's experience. She took the advice offered by (former) senior archivist Dale Couch to "think from the gut" and later came to realize that "the gut is often wiser than the head. That it's important to move on your hunches, inner feelings, and according to the compass from within."[31] For her pathbreaking research on female Georgian convict-lease prisoners, she delved deep: "Incarcerated women left no diaries. No memoirs. Very few written records at all. . . . Whipping reports was a place where their voices could be imagined. . . . I thought from my gut. I wondered why they were whipped, and what those whippings said about their refusal to be commodified and dominated. Then I wrote from within."[32] LeFlouria's impressive ability to listen and *hear* Nora Daniel, Carrie Massie, and Ella Gamble, among others, reaped reward as she wrote and garnered accolades. LeFlouria translated their stories into her prizewinning *Chained in Silence: Black Women and Convict Labor in the New South* (2015). Such stirring scholarship reflects the powerful scope of contemporary Southern women's history.[33]

The kindness of archivists—be it in giving advice or access—can change the course of many a scholar's career. Thus, one of my favorite memories took place in the 1980s, when I was working on my second book. I had been sent a copy of *The Collection of Writings by Virginia Women in the Lipscomb Library, Randolph-Macon Woman's College: A Catalog of the Collection* (first published in 1974). I had met one of their librarians at an SAWH reception at the Southern Historical Association meeting and was intrigued enough to make a detour to Lynchburg while on another trip.

This guide has given way to the digital revolution, and thus the print medium has become obsolete, but the collection goes on. A current librarian suggests that their collection "is primarily fiction and includes everything from V.C. Andrews, to Willa Cather, to local cookbooks, but does not offer a significant collection of historical writings."[34] I beg to differ.

During my research jaunt to Virginia in the 1980s, I stopped at the college to survey works featured in the catalog. I did find what I felt was *significant* historical writing, some as intriguing as I had ever encountered by that time, including privately printed volumes and obscure Virginiana. But even more enchanting, the collection was housed in a beautiful room upstairs in the college library. The door was unlocked by an archivist who showed me a desk where I could work, without an attendant in the room. I was left alone to use the collection at my own pace. I worked steadily but could not imagine how I could examine all I wanted when I had only two days. At the end of the first day, I didn't even have to ask: the librarian came to say good night when she went home at five. She told me I could stay working as long as the library remained open. Then she gave me the key—a key I could use to lock up on my own and return to the front desk as I left. I could not have been more pleased, more appreciative—a treasure trove of resources without having to break down the door!

To this day, I know more *key-givers* than *gatekeepers* in Southern libraries and archives. As the SAWH turns fifty, we will share individual and collective memories during upcoming commemorations. But one memory has stuck with me over the years.

When I took a teaching post at Harvard in 1983, I was anchored in New England—teaching, raising a family, trying to complete research and writing, with plate-spinning as a survival technique. Certainly, time was a precious commodity. I lived only minutes away from the marvelous Schlesinger Library at Radcliffe (one of the great archives in American women's history, but not exactly a rich resource for Southern women). I had an opportunity to switch allegiances and would remain in New England for another decade and a half. However, from that day working in the Lipscomb Library at Randolph-Macon Woman's College on, lingering doubts about my selection of a Southern path were banished: my instincts had been certain and right.

The puzzle of Southern women's history would continue, but I felt reassured—ringing the bells all those years, raising hell's bells along the way, unlocking stories of Southern women's histories—that the journey would lead me to this half century of tales to cherish, memories to recall, and friendships to renew.

Notes

1. *Women's History Sources: A Guide to Archives and Manuscript Collections in the United States*, ed. Andrea Hinding, Ames Sheldon Bower, and Clarke A. Chambers, in association with the University of Minnesota (New York: Bowker, 1979).

2. And indeed she still would: she shares a biography with her siblings—Lee V. Chambers's *The Weston Sisters: An American Abolitionist Family* (Chapel Hill: University of North Carolina Press, 2015) but deserves her own volume.

3. Networking with women was spectacular while other encounters were not so welcoming, which I detail elsewhere in "The Southern Social Network," *Journal of Southern History* 83, no. 1 (February 2017): 7–36.

4. See AHA newsletter, "Assessing Women's History from a Personal Angle," Mary Beth Norton, October 25, 2018.

5. Private correspondence, Sandra Treadway to Catherine Clinton, November 16, 2018, at 9:13:50 a.m. EST.

6. Email response from the South Carolina State Archives.

7. Private correspondence, Sandra Treadway to Catherine Clinton, November 16, 2018, at 9:13:50 a.m. EST.

8. George B. Tindall, "Jumping Jim Crow," in *Historians and Race: Autobiography and the Writing of History*, ed. Paul Cimbala and Robert Himmelberg (Bloomington: Indiana University Press, 1996), 7.

9. Brent Staples, "So the South's White Terror Will Never Be Forgotten," *New York Times*, April 25, 2018.

10. Haley Aaron to Nancy Dupree, email correspondence, Wednesday, September 5, 2018, 3:46 p.m.

11. Available at https://libraries.uark.edu/specialcollections/research/guides/womensstudies.asp.

12. Available at http://ahc.digital-ar.org/cdm/singleitem/collection/p16790coll13/id/288/rec/4.

13. Southern Research Report #3, prepared for the Faculty Working Group in Southern Studies of the University of North Carolina at Chapel Hill with support from the Institute for Research in Social Science and the Southern Historical Collection, 4–5.

14. Southern Research Report #3, 16.

15. Available at https://docsouth.unc.edu/sohp/women.html.

16. Available at https://guides.library.duke.edu/subject/womens-sexuality-studies.

17. Correspondence between Katherine Walters and Yuki Hibben, September 19, 2018, at 12:33:18 p.m. CDT.

18. Correspondence between Katherine Walters and Eileen Paris, August 30, 2018, at 2:35:47 p.m. CDT.

19. (Richmond, Va.: 1996).

20. See http://vaheritage.org/.

21. Correspondence between Katherine Walters and Jennifer McGillan, September 17, 2018, at 9:27:58 AM CDT. Available at https://www.lib.lsu.edu/special/manuscripts/guides/women as does Mississippi; http://lib.msstate.edu/specialcollections/collections/manuscripts/women/.

22. See, for example, Catherine Clinton and Emily West, "Gender and Sexuality in the Old South," in *Reinterpreting Southern* History, ed. Craig Friend and Lorri Glover (Baton Rouge: Louisiana State University Press, 2020).

23. Jim Downs, "The Other Side of Freedom: Destitution, Disease and Dependency among Freedwomen and Their Children During and After the Civil War," in *Battle Scars: Race, Gender and Sexuality During the Civil War*, ed. Catherine Clinton and Nina Silber (New York: Oxford University Press, 2005).

24. Private correspondence between Erica Armstrong Dunbar and Catherine Clinton, January 13, 2019.

25. Private correspondence between Erica Armstrong Dunbar and Catherine Clinton, January 13, 2019.

26. Private correspondence between Erica Armstrong Dunbar and Catherine Clinton, January 13, 2019.

27. Private correspondence between Ðaina Ramey Berry and Catherine Clinton, January 29, 2019.

28. Private correspondence between Daina Ramey Berry and Catherine Clinton, January 29, 2019.

29. Private correspondence between Daina Ramey Berry and Catherine Clinton, January 29, 2019.

30. Private correspondence between Tiya Miles and Catherine Clinton, November 30, 2018.

31. Private correspondence between Talithia LeFlouria and Catherine Clinton, January 29, 2019.

32. Private correspondence between Talithia LeFlouria and Catherine Clinton, January 29, 2019.

33. See Catherine Clinton and Emily West, "Gender and Sexuality in the Old South," in *Reinterpreting Southern Histories*, ed. Craig Thompson Friend and Lorri Glover (Baton Rouge: Louisiana University Press, 2019).

34. Email from Randolph College (renamed in 2007 from Randolph-Macon Woman's College).

2

Testing Our Mettle

Women's and Gender History in the Battle over the Civil War

MICHELE GILLESPIE

The Civil War tested the mettle of hundreds of thousands of soldiers on one battlefield after another across four arduous years. Historians have long documented the courage and resilience of those men who demonstrated tenacity in the face of terrible hardship.[1] While women's and gender historians over the last fifty years have not suffered such physical horrors, they have had to test their mettle on the scholarly battlefield of Civil War history. Theirs has been a dogged fight in the face of strong opposition to gendering a past that traditional historians and popular culture have preferred to see as great battles between great men. Newer narratives that document white and black women's resistance, agency, and leadership across the Civil War era have been contesting these persistent older accounts for several decades. Recently historians have disputed traditional historical approaches even more rigorously by exposing the cultural meanings of gender during wartime. They have argued that ideas about masculinity and femininity shaped Civil War political discourse, social thought, and economic roles, ultimately affecting the nature and outcome of the war. The Southern Association for Women Historians (SAWH) has long been a critical locus of support for these scholars who are challenging outmoded conceptions of the Civil War that emanate from within the profession and across mainstream American media and culture.

In our post-Trump election, post-truth, maybe even post-history world, it may seem naive to want women's and gender history, in all its complexity, to be more fully incorporated into the history of the American Civil War.[2] Yet I am especially worried that the eye-opening, voluminous work on Civil War–era Southern white and black women and gender has become increasingly disposable in our current moment. Despite being heralded for its fertile interrogation of the sources and its analytical brio, this big body of scholarship is too often considered a subfield. The arguments in these often brilliant books are still not regularly and consistently referenced in the field as a whole, and certainly not in the popular American histories that purport to cover the Civil War. This essay argues that historians must transform their teaching and writing about the Civil War by centering Southern women's and gender history in the narrative. It also celebrates the SAWH for supporting so many of the scholars who have launched these important correctives. Indeed, I wonder if the next big challenge for the Southern Association for Women Historians is not so much generating more great histories of Southern women, gender, and sexuality but ensuring that this scholarship is in fact less sidelined and more integrated, both in popular history and in those powerful spaces—academic departments, associations, journals, presses, conferences, foundations, and prize committees—where scholarly Civil War history is debated, crafted, and critiqued.

It is important to set this growing body of important work against the backdrop of more than sixty thousand books that attempt to capture the political thought, military design, and social turmoil of the Civil War. The most popular narrative that emerges from all this general scholarship celebrates the Civil War for preserving the Union and thwarting America's racist past by ending slavery. Paul Escott has recently challenged that narrative, stating that our current politically and socially splintered world is a sharp reminder that we may be better served articulating the Civil War's failures over its successes. He maintains that Civil War studies are at "an inflection point." The field must generate fresher understandings by applying new methods of analysis and innovative approaches.[3] Using women's history and gender history to evaluate the Civil War does just that, by transforming how we understand it. The making of confederate nationalism, of what constitutes "battlefields" and who fought on them, and of the power of historical actors long invisible to traditional historians looks wholly different with gendered perspectives.

The Civil War freed 4 million enslaved men, women, and children, preserved the Union, and brought enormous changes to U.S. government and society. Over the course of the war, the South transmuted itself into one enormous military and domestic battlefield. As many as one million Southerners fought for the Confederacy and more than a quarter of them died, along with fifty thousand civilians. In this fractured society in constant motion, half a million slaves escaped to Union lines, Confederate families fled in advance of the Union Army, deserters returned to their kin, and guerrilla warfare reigned to the west.

The impact of this wartime chaos on Southern white women would not be addressed by historians until more than a hundred years after the Civil War itself, although it was documented in dozens and dozens of women's memoirs. It would take Mary Elizabeth Massey to write, in the aftermath of the Civil War centennial, about wives fighting with their husbands over whether to stay in their homes and about refugee women struggling to support their families. Indeed, Massey's work was so formative that *Civil War History* devoted a forum to the current state of women's history in honor of the fiftieth anniversary of *Bonnet Brigades: American Women in the Civil War* (1966). As that journal issue demonstrates, with its probing essays by prominent women's historians, Massey's work foreshadowed what would ultimately become an avalanche of new scholarship not only on women's wartime experience and agency but also on the power of gendered analysis to transform our understanding of the Civil War past.[4]

We have learned much over the last fifty years: the degree to which white women and children fended for themselves, becoming widows and orphans at alarming rates; how Confederate-ruled cities turned into menacing disaster zones for women of all ages and social classes where they were forced to confront inflation, desperate mobs, and starvation; and the cruel effect of marauding armies burning crops, homes, farms, churches, and schools, when they did not appropriate them, putting women and children in dangerous straits. Women's lives were rocked by Union occupation with the imposition of curfews, confiscation, and even exile, and cold-blooded guerrilla warfare brought a new kind of battlefield to their front doors. But through all these disasters, some women—Massey called them "Southern women of invention," Drew Faust would call them "mothers of invention"—were finding new opportunities for themselves, whether through organizing food riots or entering new professions, striking for higher wages or running plantations and farms.[5]

In the wake of new histories of slavery in the 1970s, and the influence of women's and gendered history in the 1980s and 1990s, scholars began to document at long last enslaved and freedwomen's experiences too, and that body of scholarship has become a promising force in more recent years especially. This new work shows how badly black women and children suffered in wartime, separated from their families by fleeing planters and by army impressment, their bodies subject to at least as raced violence and abuse as in the antebellum period. This growing literature also demonstrates that even if enslaved women managed to escape to Union lines, they became contraband, treated like prisoners and exploited therein too. Uncertainty, scarcity, and want on top of brutality made the Civil War lives of African American women a living hell, although they also fought for and secured agency and opportunity and would grow their leadership throughout emancipation and Reconstruction.[6]

With the publication of field-defining works like Catherine Clinton and Nina

Silber's anthology *Divided Houses: Gender and the Civil War* (1992), successive generations of women's historians have depicted the varied ways in which women, whether enslaved, working-class, or elite, fashioned new identities for themselves and launched telling political critiques across the wartime South. This work put women literally at the battle scene, as nurses, spies, soldiers, prostitutes, laundresses, and refugees, even as it explored the ways women on the home front fought wars within their households to keep their social status, ideological beliefs, and soldier sons alive. This scholarship has demonstrated that Southern white women's nationalistic support of the Civil War shaped Union Army strategy from the beginning, substituting more often than not the home front for the battlefield in what is a powerful reenvisioning of how we locate the war and its impact. Union armies destroyed the households of their enemies in the Mississippi Valley, and Sherman evicted the women and children of Atlanta precisely because of the challenge they posed to Union success. Meanwhile, gendered understandings in the American South were radically altered by the acute crisis of experiencing the war, and all its attendant consequences, as Southern society reorganized in post-Emancipation. Southern women, elite, poor, and enslaved, fought hard to construct and claim their citizenship. African American women fought hard for freedom and emancipation at the confluence of military action, policy making, and civil courts.[7]

All this transformative research that has snowballed over the last fifty years *should* be remaking the way historians understand the Civil War, as well as the way the public perceives it, especially in the wake of the sesquicentennial. The question we need to ask ourselves is whether that has really been happening and what still needs to be done to ensure that it does. This query is not meant to challenge the work of the SAWH but instead to underline its importance and suggest a renewed marshalling of its efforts. Although there have been multiple intellectual, social, and political wellsprings that help explain the outpouring of so much great Southern women's and gender history over the last five decades, the SAWH has been an especially mighty buttress for this work and a strong advocate for its integration into mainstream fields. All the more reason why we need its ongoing support in the battle over the national narratives of the Civil War.

I did not always think this way. Like all of us who have been in the field for a long time, I increasingly find myself documenting my personal intellectual narrative alongside the larger currents in our profession. As I think about the profound importance of assimilating the battlefields of the home front with traditional military battlefields, I am struck by my tardiness at arriving at this conclusion, even as I look to and applaud the scholars and leaders of the SAWH, so many of whom work in this Civil War field, for getting me there;

I suspect my journey is not that dissimilar to some others. Five decades ago, a handful of women historians who were attending the Southern Historical Association (SHA) meeting gathered in the basement of the Kentucky Hotel in Louisville next to the boiler room. While these women were organizing a caucus to study the status of women in the profession and encourage women's history scholarship, I was reading books by the popular Civil War historian Bruce Catton, oblivious, as a ten-year-old in New Jersey, to the absence of women and slavery in these volumes.[8] By the time I entered college, scholars across the 1970s had been scouring archives for women's voices and were publishing new books challenging male-centric narratives of eighteenth- and nineteenth-century American history. At Rice University I read Anne Scott's *Southern Lady* and C. Vann Woodward's *Mary Chesnut's Civil War* in John Boles's classes, and I also read the new scholarship on the history of U.S. slavery and slave culture with him.[9] Eager to contribute to the ways women's and enslaved people's inclusion in U.S. history narratives would change how we understood the past, I had the good fortune of working as the student assistant for the *Journal of Southern History* (*JSH*), where I learned how history was made through the review process. It was there that I also learned how young women historians like Catherine Clinton, Suzanne Lebsock, Jacqueline Jones, and Thavolia Glymph were beginning to reshape Southern history, largely based on the reports that John Boles, as the new *JSH* editor, was bringing back to the staff from the annual SHA meetings, and I found their work absolutely inspiring. What I was much less aware of, because I received so much support from my professors at Rice to become a historian, was how *few* women were publishing and succeeding professionally in Southern history at that time. In fact, during my first year of college (1979–1980), women constituted only 13 percent of the *JSH* board of editors, none of the authors, and only 8 percent of the book reviewers. John Boles became editor in 1981 and began changing these numbers, growing women's board membership to 25 percent, women's authorship to 8 percent, and women book reviewers to 19 percent by 1985 and helping to create a critical report analyzing longer-term gender trends within the SHA and the *JSH*.[10]

I left Rice for graduate school at Princeton University eager to do Southern history that integrated women's history and the history of slavery. At Princeton, I learned about the fabulous new work in gender history led by French historian Natalie Davis with her coterie of impressive grad students. Joan Scott was part of that community through the Institute for Advanced Study preparing what would be her groundbreaking essay on gender and the politics of history. I was dumbstruck by the implications of all this work; it made me challenge what I had come to see as my too-simple understanding of U.S. and Southern history. As I prepared for my qualifying exams, one in early America, one in U.S. women's history, and one in nineteenth-century America, I felt I still lacked the theoretical finesse to be a good historian, but I did grasp that race and gender were powerful social constructs and that to be a good historian meant teasing out and explaining the context behind their shaping in different places and times. All the while, I was developing a thesis topic with Civil War historian James McPherson and yet was still ignoring how largely absent women and gender were from the field of Civil War history itself, probably because I had tunnel vision and was more interested in the social, political, and cultural history of the antebellum years and the ways women's and gender history was reshaping that field.

What turned the corner for me was joining the SAWH as a graduate student. Suddenly, I found myself among a group of like-minded scholars, at all stages of their careers, asking similar questions, doing exciting work, and eager to talk about their findings, methods, and theory. This community of scholars was a force with which to be reckoned. Its members knew how to run an up-and-coming organization. They wrote good history, and they wanted to support more history writing and more female scholars doing the writing. They used their talents as planners, implementers, and fundraisers to hold annual meetings and conferences, to offer scholarship prizes, and to produce book series, and they evolved into an ever-expanding network of generous scholars. There was an important synergy at play here; the best scholars in Southern women's and gender history were invariably also SAWH leaders. I saw them doing professional work and I read their books, and they were both intellectual and career models for me.

What distinguished these women-led SAWH events, formal and informal, from other organizations and conferences was their commitment to welcoming everyone, from all schools, whether community colleges or the Ivies, and to supporting historians, whether in grad school or retirement. While these meetings did not reflect attendance that was particularly racially or ethnically diverse early on in my experience, the need to do better on this front, the need to be more inclusive, was always a central conversation and voiced long before other organizations did so, at least in my memory. The SAWH was also the first place in the profession where I heard issues like sexual harassment and gender discrimination discussed openly and seriously. It was also the first and last conference to which I ever brought an infant child. While I knew that all my colleagues empathized with my predicament as a brand-new working mother fulfilling my committee expectations by attending, I quickly discovered, as Virginia Woolf articulated long ago, that women's experiences are too often bodied ones. The SAWH has long since sought to provide childcare at conferences whenever possible.[11]

Equally important, the SAWH created a professional space in which scholars of Southern women's history and gender could name, share, and legitimate the challenges they were often facing as historians, including condescension about their subject choice and its intellectual merits and skepticism about the availability of "suitable" archival resources. It was at SAWH events, from panel discussions to late-night conversations, where we could voice our frustration at the absence of women's and especially African American women's voices, actions, and lived experiences in the Southern past but also in our own present. It was here that I listened to compelling stories about the very real professional challenges of researching and writing women's and gender history, especially in the male-centric, military history–oriented Civil War field.

The SAWH has been a place that legitimizes historians' desire to find agency in that half of the population that had been hidden from history for two thousand years. It also, and just as importantly, has always given agency to young female scholars seeking to be professional historians. My SAWH work also explains my willingness to do administrative work at this stage of my career. I know I am making a difference in a university where women's leadership has long been limited. While the SAWH has made many singular contributions to its members and the profession, one of the most vital has been its insistence on women's equity in the profession. From policies to annual addresses, conference keynotes, grad student workshops, and roundtables, and from the 1970s right down to the present, the SAWH has always called for more gender equity. It has encouraged women to go willingly into traditional male preserves of power, as thesis advisers, panel chairs, journal reviewers and board members, organization presidents, department chairs and deans.[12] That women's equity in higher ed remains a challenge is borne out in a recent study that documented that while 52 percent of lecturers are women, only 24 percent are full professors, 14 percent department chairs, and 12 percent deans. It should be no surprise that the numbers of women of color in these more senior posts fall well below these already modest figures.[13]

While the SAWH has staunchly championed women's professional status, and many of its members have gone on to lead other organizations like the SHA and the Organization of American Historians, to lead departments and colleges and even Harvard University, and to lead movements like the Cassandra Project, the organization has been first and foremost an advocate for important new scholarship.[14] By the 1990s, SAWH officers, keynote speakers, and the membership itself were publishing field-changing books and articles.

The triennial conference had quickly evolved into the "go to" event for younger scholars eager to get feedback from the top scholars in the field. The University Press of Missouri partnered with the SAWH to publish a series on Southern women's history based on the best SAWH conference papers, up to nine volumes now, and the SAWH book and article prizes garner serious attention. Just in the last decade the University of Georgia Press has published a new state-by-state series of biographical essays about significant women that currently covers ten states, for a total of nineteen volumes. Virtually all the editors are SAWH members, and almost all the authors too. All told, the SAWH has become a key intellectual locus where bold new work that challenges once rigid presumptions about the limits of source material has recovered the ways women across race, class, and place have made their mark on the Southern past. But for all its remarkable successes, and for all the ways it has championed women's academic leadership in all its forms, it has the capacity to press for even more transformation, especially in one of the last bastions of traditional U.S. history: the American Civil War.

This is not to say that the growth of women's history and gender history of the Civil War has been anything but remarkable. A journey across the unfolding of this scholarship over the last three decades discloses exceptional imagination and tenacity. While women's and gender historians were combing the letters and memoirs of Southern slaveholding women and debating the extent of their cultural and social power in the antebellum South, and while Ken Burns was reaping a huge viewership and many kudos for his PBS Civil War documentary (1990) in which women received short shrift, Catherine Clinton and Nina Silber were putting together a pioneering collection, *Divided Houses: Gender and the Civil War* (1992), that showed how the Civil War transformed gender roles and attitudes toward sexuality among Americans across race and class in both the North and the South. The authors of these essays, many of whom were young scholars who would publish important monographs and lead distinguished careers thereafter, demonstrated how gender analysis could illuminate everything about the Civil War, from political tensions to military resistance, in profoundly new ways.

The essays were important and exciting, but as is often the case in new fields, they offered the possibility of a new read on Civil War history more than an outright new interpretation. LeeAnn Whites's *The Civil War as a Crisis in Gender*, published three years later, would do just that.[15] Offering up impressive theoretical insight, Whites documented changing gender relationships during the Civil War. Based on her analysis of Augusta, Georgia, she showed how Southern ideology justified going to war to defend the liberties of free men but then later argued that men fought the war to protect their women and children. At the same time, these very same women and children did not feel protected at all; they suffered miserably and as a result reinvented themselves outside traditional gender roles in the midst of a terrible crisis that the Confederate leadership controlled only with rhetoric. Drew Faust took that argument to the next level. In *Mothers of Invention* (1996), she argued that Southern women found so much fault with their devastating material circumstances as well as the ideological objectives of the Confederacy that they intentionally undermined the effectiveness of the South's military and economic efforts from deep within the Confederate state.[16]

These powerful contributions and others like them during the 1990s, all calling for a broadening of what constituted Civil War history that went well beyond battlefields and generals, laid the groundwork for the increasingly sophisticated and closely grained gendered work on the Civil War era that appeared across the 2000s. It began with rich new scholarship on civilians and communities, not the least of which was the important Edward Ayers–led collaborative digital project, Valley of the Shadow, on citizens in two communities, one Unionist, one Confederate, in the Shenandoah Valley, across the Civil War.[17] This new community work with its detailed fresh local studies approach, examined relationships between soldiers and their families on the home front and changing attitudes toward race and gender. This fresh attention to the impact of war on civilian life documented the hitherto woefully overlooked fact that the Civil War was as disruptive on the home front as on the battlefield.[18]

Emblematic of the best of this new generation's work is Amy Murrell Taylor's finely wrought *The Divided Family in Civil War America* (2009). The war divided more than brothers, she argues. It divided all family members and had powerful repercussions for postwar America. Taylor showed how families worked assiduously to frame issues such as slavery and secession with domestic, gendered categories like duty, authority, and generation, but ultimately to no avail. They could not keep politics and family separate despite their staunchest efforts to secure their own mental succor by invoking their Victorian ideology of public and private spheres. Battle lines across the nation meant divided families, however hard families fought to keep their gendered notions of households and their privacy intact. These kinds of examinations of the effects of war on family relations have led to critical new scholarship about the Confederacy. They are important in their own right even as they strike another powerful blow against the traditional emphasis on military and political history as the sum total of Civil War history.[19]

Other critical new work centers on the documenting of a confederate nationalism that took shape at wartime but would be refashioned into a particular Civil War memory for years thereafter. Anne Sarah Rubin's *A Shattered Nation* (2007) eloquently depicts a confederate nationalism constructed not by political leaders and heroes on the battlefield but by ordinary men and women out of their lived experience in wartime and their emotional need for explanation and healing.[20] Similarly, by raking through the Civil War–era archives of the complicated border state of Kentucky, Anne Marshall, in *Creating a Confederate Kentucky* (2010), adeptly explains white women's subsequent construction of their Civil War memory, a complex, contested, and unpredictable memorialization of the lost Confederate generation and the emancipation of slaves.[21]

Into this space of gender as social construct once again stepped Catherine Clinton and Nina Silber with another stunning collection, *Battle Scars* (2006). This volume brought together provocative essays that did not simply document a broader range of the experiences of men and women in wartime. They explored how cultural and ideological systems in flux in the midst of war could reshape male and female behavior, gender roles, and raced behavior depending on the context. The anthology taken as a whole contends that socially sanctioned patterns of gender behavior and masculine and feminine ideals were transformed across the Civil War era, especially as white Southern men dealt with defeat and freedmen and women sought to determine their own identity and future in emancipation.

This gendered approach necessitates reassessment of all traditional presumptions. The extreme loss of life on the battlefield—likely more than 700,000 soldiers—has long drawn popular attention, but this gendered work underscores the need to analyze the psychological impact of all that suffering on survivors too.[22] This fuller context gives the familiar wartime topics of violence and death important new meanings. Drew Faust, in her 2008 book on death and the Civil War, *This Republic of Suffering*, studied how Americans struggled to make sense of this unprecedented carnage. Confronting death of that magnitude changed the nation, she contends, generating new systems of civic and federal policies and responsibilities. Through the voices of women and freedpeople, not just the male leaders of the time, the book underscores the victimization of all civilians, slave and free, male and female, as they endured starvation, massive displacement, rampant disease, and many other forms of violence and abuse.

In her pathbreaking book, *Rape and Race in the Nineteenth-Century South*, Diane Miller Sommerville documented the ways the Southern legal system and white Southerners dealt with rape across the long Civil War era. She argued that white Southerners' fears of black rape were constructed late in the nineteenth century, not during the slave South. In the antebellum era, she found great fluidity across racial and sexual lines, and more tolerance among whites for intimacy between black men and white women even during the Civil War as the slave system split apart. Somerville concluded that race was not the most salient social hierarchy in the South.[23] In fact, poor white women were cast as the most depraved and despised in this surprisingly changeable world, as Victoria Bynum had documented earlier in her notable book, *Unruly Women*. Stephanie McCurry picked up this thread by looking at the political and social maelstrom of Confederate contestation created by the war. She emphasized that poor white women, often soldiers' wives, joined farmers, slaves, generals, and soldiers to fight over control of the Confederacy's resources. These women and African American women gained new kinds of authority and a whole new political stage that politicians could not ignore. The image of the long-suffering loyal soldier's wife looked ludicrous against large numbers of women present-ing petitions and pleas in search of relief and launching bread riots in Atlanta, Richmond, and Salisbury. This internal violence and turmoil, argues McCurry, was just the tip of the iceberg, as more and more women and slaves built new networks that facilitated more extensive political actions against the Confeder-ate guard.[24]

Scholars using women's and gendered history to expose the social and po-litical disorder of the home front force us to remake older, narrower narratives of the Civil War. If some of this work indicates working women's resistance against the Confederacy and even alignment with African American inter-ests, other work suggests that elite white women embraced the Confederate cause and made it their own. Perhaps no group of scholars has been better able to bring this point home than those who have applied gender analysis to Sherman's March at the end of the war. In *When Sherman Marched to the Sea*, Jacquelyn Glass Campbell uses evidence from Northern soldiers and South-ern civilians, black and white, male and female, to show how Sherman's men invaded the Southern elite white woman's home literally and psychologically. Northern soldiers, who considered commandeering Southern households their military duty, were shocked by the force with which many white Southern women defended their households. For Campbell, such bravery made manifest white women's material and ideological need for defiance and launched white women's vital new role as bona fide citizens in the Confederate nation.[25]

Lisa Frank, in her exciting book *The Civilian War*, goes even further by put-ting Southern women at the forefront of the war once the Union army marched across Georgia and the Carolinas. That march, she argues, must be under-stood as "a gender-specific military campaign," one in which elite slaveholding women were the Union Army's political targets. Frank makes clear that these women fought back hard and saw themselves as working assiduously on behalf of the Confederacy, confirming their stake in the new nation with a feminized nationalism. Sherman exploited women's commitment by using it to legitimize his making them into combatants. Frank also posits that this extreme turn of events emasculated Confederate soldiers unable to protect their women and children in their homes.[26] This relationship between emasculation and suffering deserves deeper exploration. Recent work by Diane Somerville, Catherine Clinton, and others has explored the trauma of war on Confederate soldiers imbued in a masculine code of honor that they could not meet and that can be measured by an uptick in suicides.[27]

Much of this work has emphasized the white Confederacy and the complex gender relations of white men and women, but gender scholars have also been turning their attention to slaveholding men and women. Leslie Schwalm, in her pioneering *A Hard Fight for We* (1998), revealed the myriad ways African American women fought for their freedom during and after the war and the ways they sought to redefine their life and labor in low country South Carolina.[28] Critically important new work is beginning to uncover more experiences of African American women during and in the immediate aftermath of wartime. It is documenting a world not only of enslaved women fighting for their freedom but one of horrific neglect, starvation, outright sexual terror, and despair.[29] Amy Murrell Taylor, in *Embattled Freedom* (2018), offers the first synthetic history of the wartime refugees, some hundreds of thousands of enslaved men and women, by truly integrating military and social history.[30] In a mass exodus that destroyed the institution of slavery from inside the heart of the Confederacy, enslaved people fled dangerous home fronts to reach the battlefronts where they sought freedom and citizenship in army-supervised contraband camps. Despite these heroic efforts, women experienced particular abuse and terror in them. Crystal Feimster has detailed the extent of white officer rape of black women in these sites.[31] In what she has called an "archive of sorrow," Thavolia Glymph has documented the gruesome and dehumanizing hardships enslaved women endured in wartime, from the trauma of displaced and cruelly separated families to their horrendous treatment in the refugee camps. The scholars insist that the "disremembering" of these women's sufferings and the historical invisibility of their struggles and lasting traumas demands our reconciliation, at least as much as the ubiquitous military casualty lists and war memorials.[32]

The SAWH has been a critical source of support through its conferences, panels, and annual addresses for this outpouring of exceptional new work.

Interestingly, however, only five of the thirty-nine SAWH annual addresses (12 percent) delivered at the SHA since 1979 have covered the Civil War period, although each of these five speakers subsequently published one or more field redefining, award-winning articles or books on this era: Catherine Clinton delivered "Sex and the Sectional Conflict" in 1990; Thavolia Glymph, "Civil War Memoirs and the Reinvention of Black Women's History" in 1993; Stephanie McCurry, "'The Brothers' War'? Free Women, Slaves, and Popular Politics in the Civil War 'South'" in 1999; Jacqueline Jones, "Nancy Johnson's Story: Rethinking the History of Women in the South During the Civil War and Reconstruction" in 2005; and Crystal Feimster, "'Indecent and Obscene': White Officers, Black Women, and Rape in the 'Contraband Quarters' of the American Civil War" in 2012.

It is important that the SAWH continue to step into the fray. In 2015, at the tenth SAWH Conference held in Charleston in 2015, a big roundtable titled "The Civil War as a Household War," with discussants including Civil War historians LeeAnn Whites, Lisa Frank, and Margaret M. Storey, asserted the centrality of the home front to any understanding of Civil War history. Three years later, at the eleventh SAWH Conference, held in Tuscaloosa, some half dozen authors read papers on Civil War women's and gender history, and another roundtable titled "Defining the Field of Battle: Gender and the Civil War," with LeeAnn Whites and Lisa Frank again, and also Barbara Gannon, Judith Giesberg, and Amy Taylor, insisted on the need to gender how we conceptualize all aspects of Civil War history and redefine how scholars understand the battlefront. Recently, the culmination of this important work resulted in Frank and Whites publishing *Household War: How Americans Lived and Fought the Civil War* (Athens: University of Georgia Press, 2020).

The SAWH is generating a new kind of intellectual energy through these rigorous conversations and the empowerment they generate for scholars and audiences alike. At the same time, the hardest act for the SAWH and its membership to engage in going forward will be persuading scholars outside the SAWH who are reluctant to acknowledge these new ways of thinking about the Civil War.

Our broader culture does not seem to be much help here. Given the growing momentum of this cutting-edge work, it is difficult to look at popular depictions of the Civil War and not get a little crazed. A simple googling of the Wikipedia Civil War entry, or pulling up the Civil War–themed commentary and archived stories in the *New York Times*, would lead one to conclude that half the population of the South never existed. In her smart book of essays *Dead Girls*, Alice Bolin observes all the ways media and print culture have used America's obsession with abused, tortured, maimed, and murdered young women and their bodies as backdrops for telling men's stories since the mid-twentieth-century, from Raymond Chandler's film noir to the endless supply of *Law and Order* episodes.[33] I am being flip, but I would almost prefer that popular depictions of the Civil War at least begin their narratives with "the 'dead girls' motif" rather than leave women out altogether.

In short, contemporary American media still prefers narratives about fallen soldiers and battles lost, omitting the stories historians have been recovering about women and children who suffered the loss of loved ones and who were in essence "sentenced to live" with their sadness. If James McPherson is right in calling the American Civil War "the central event in America's historical consciousness," would not media acknowledgment of the Civil War as a history of assault and trauma *for the civilians* who fought multiple wars at home across gender, race, and class generate new empathy? Would it also not invite new questions about inequity, suffering, and pain in our present world? Judith Giesberg has recently suggested that the work of this new cadre of historians, all of which sheds powerful new light on the experiences of wartime women and children on the home front as its own battlefield, may have gone too far, by privileging civilians over soldiers.[34] But I would argue that until the American public grasps this conception of widespread civilian suffering and resistance, we have not gone far enough. In fact, in our own historical moment, where political polarization, violence, racism, and economic disparity predominate, we should dig even deeper into civilians' emotional lives, including the psychological impact of the traumas they faced, as in the work addressing rape and suicide and in the work of Alisha Hines, who, in showing how enslaved women used the Mississippi River as a series of liberating spaces for their empowerment, highlights overlooked avenues of resistance.[35]

So how is the SAWH and its membership going to make sure that this exciting work is more fully integrated into Civil War history—and I mean the history that historians write and the history that popular media distributes. To our fellow historians, we have to ask why too few articles in each regular issue integrate gendered analysis? Why can't the editors and reviewers use the peer review process to insist that submitted articles do just that? I recently served on a prize committee for a best journal article. We read and then discussed the merits of some two and a half dozen essays published over the previous two years. One of the essays situated itself in the Civil War–era South, and it was a smart, original, well-argued, well-written essay. In fact, it was one of the top three essays on each of the committee members' lists. But in the end, we agreed not to award it the prize. While it was very good, it reflected no women's or gendered historiography or interpretation whatsoever, treating the enslaved people it was discussing as undifferentiated by sex or gender. It was as if years of rich scholarship on this topic had never existed.

One might argue that we were being unfair, choosing to eliminate the essay because of what it did not do, rather than what it did and did well. But here's the rub, and here's where we as historians have to be more scrupulous and more demanding: the essay essentially ignored the unique experiences of half of its subjects, and it ignored splendid scholarship that would have profoundly deepened the author's analysis. This selective amnesia reflects persistent bias.

Over twenty years ago, Glenda Gilmore in her SAWH address critiqued the walling off of scholarship into disciplinary subfields, describing this inclination as the balkanization of history. For Gilmore, "analyses that separate these subfields misrepresent the way people actually lived their lives."[36] Until we hold our colleagues accountable for their tendency to balkanize women's and gender history, we are not being good historians. If we in the profession had been fair to the author whose otherwise good essay ignored gender, the author would have received that critique during the peer review process. So we have to ask ourselves why that did not happen and figure out how to make that happen more.

No scholar has worked harder to challenge that balkanization across the course of her impressive career than Catherine Clinton. A leading historian, and a prolific one, she has been an extraordinary advocate for and contributor to the gendered rethinking of the history of the American Civil War. Her important books, essays, edited collections, and invited lectures, along with her generous mentoring of younger scholars, have always insisted on documenting the presence, voices, viewpoints, and contributions of white and black women during the Civil War era across class and place. Her inexhaustible scholarship consistently demands rethinking women's roles, whether she is reenvisioning Harriet Tubman's life work, exploring Mary Lincoln's psyche, explaining the construction of the plantation legend in the wake of Confederate defeat, bringing the debates over Confederate monuments into the headlines, or providing critical context for understanding Susie King Taylor's ordeals as a former slave working in army camps.[37]

But what else can we be doing besides generating exciting new work? Stephanie McCurry's latest book, *Women's War: Fighting and Surviving the American Civil War*, offers one of the first synthetic looks at women's centrality to the Civil War in the wake of this new scholarship, arguing that women played a profoundly transformative role in the Civil War on and off the battlefield. She shows how white and black women defied authority, Confederate and Union, and made their own paths toward greater autonomy and freedom. She insists that the war, emancipation, and economic loss changed the nature of family across race and shows how women remade the family during reconstruction. There is great value in writing a one-volume book that captures the research and arguments of dozens of historians over the past decades and is accessible, smart, and well-written.[38] But does it carry enough weight to compel new Civil War narratives? Probably not.

In Jill Lepore's chapter on the Civil War in *These Truths*, the author does something rather groundbreaking. She gives Southern women the agency Southern women's historians have long been documenting, which is not so new, but she does so in a new space—a single volume history of the United States.[39] She describes the effect of the Confederate draft on Southern families. She shows how Southern women dealt with deprivation. She points out the irony of Southern war rhetoric urging soldiers to fight to protect their wives against the backdrop of women's political protests against conscription and hunger. She underlines the fact that their wartime disfranchisement compelled Confederate white women to claim their citizenship. Lepore insists, and she can do so because she is standing atop a powerful body of scholarship across the last fifty years, that the origin of America's modern welfare state lies in Southern white women's protests during the Confederacy.

Reading McCurry's synthesis of Civil War women's and gender history, and then reading Lepore's chapter in the first one-volume U.S. history textbook authored by a woman, prompts me to share a new hope for the future of Civil War scholarship. Thirty years ago, James McPherson published *Battle Cry of Freedom*, the one-volume narrative history of the Civil War that earned him a Pulitzer Prize. At the time, reviewers raved about the book's well-written integration of political, social and military events from the war with Mexico through Appomattox, as well as its insistence on slavery as the underlying cause of the war. They celebrated the book's portrayal of emancipation, this "new birth of freedom" as Lincoln called it, as the most important legacy of America's ghastliest war. Imagine with me what a new Pulitzer Prize–winning, one-volume narrative of the Civil War would look like, one that truly integrated political, military, social, and gendered scholarship? It would be a revisionist work that fully embraces the splendid scholarship of the last five decades in women's history and histories of gender and sexuality. It would claim new intellectual territory, and it would have big repercussions for how we help the public reinterpret the Civil War.

I think the public may be hungrier for this work than the media or even we scholars realize. In the wake of the sesquicentennial, attendance at Civil

War sites was uneven and unimpressive. Some experts have surmised this was because many sites made slavery and the experiences of the enslaved more central to their interpretation at a time unfortunately when we as a society have become divided on the depths of contemporary racism as slavery's legacy. But experts have not commented on a surprising set of high visitor numbers for a few key sites. The Clara Barton National Historic Site, the Women's Rights National Historical Park, and the Maggie L. Walker National Park Site experienced dramatic increases in visitors, and two of these three sites were actually among the top five most heavily visited, not the traditional battlefields. Public historians recognize this hunger for more women's and gendered history, and they are bringing new gendered interpretations to their traditional sites.[40] We as scholars can support their efforts by writing Civil War histories that eschew balkanization and more fully capture all Southerners' experiences.

As women's and gender historians, we are always rolling up our sleeves and looking for what Anne Scott has called "unfinished business." We must balance our embrace of our expertise with a willingness to question our authoritative voice and recognize its limitations. Ironically enough, Gary Gallagher, Barton Myers, and other Civil War historians have argued that we must expunge the "mental barriers" that separate military history from political and social developments. We must likewise expunge the mental barriers that separate military, political, and social history from gendered developments.[41] It is in that light that I offer suggestions for the new kind of work I would like to see in that single-volume Civil War history.

I appreciate the recent pathbreaking "big" histories that transform the benign stories of American capitalism's triumph into a much truer depiction of national dependence on enslaved bodies to make great wealth. In these histories, the Civil War becomes a clash of market-owning titans in the North and the South, not a morality fight over slavery. But as learned and persuasive as these big histories are, as humane as they seek to be, their inattentiveness to the forces of gender seems striking and begs more focus. We also need more work on the nature of nationalism in the South on the eve of the Civil War that teases out differences across the region, between wealthy slaveholders and nonslaveholders, and between intellectual leaders, and that includes Confederate women as the ideological leaders that they were. What forces were shaping the meaning that Southerners made out of the concept of nation, and what did it mean that they were so heavily gendered? We have tended to study women's proslavery rhetoric in isolation, as an entity unto itself, but what happens when we look for new patterns of thought across the gender divide? Does the evolution of Southern nationalism begin to look different?[42]

What about Southern religion across wartime? How did religious leadership respond to home-front circumstances that fundamentally challenged the very racial and gendered hierarchies ministers had long sought to preserve? How were women from different social classes and in different places within the South making sense of their own wartime religious experience? What about the black church and women's leadership therein? Elsa Barkley Brown, Evelyn Higginbotham, and others have begun those important inquiries, but can we explore them in more detail and even link them to other forms of black women's wartime resistance?

Similarly, scholars since Stephen Channing have long documented the crisis of white fear that prevailed across Secession and the Civil War. We know from Stephen Hahn and others that enslaved men and women were well aware of the developing sectional conflict and used that knowledge to generate new means of opposition. To what extent were these information networks of knowledge and rumor gendered, and where did those places of shared intelligence across the race line mostly occur? Now that we have more studies of black women during the Civil War, we need to convey more fully how their political ideas shaped social and political realities across the Confederacy. As Laura Edwards and others have argued, internal turmoil profoundly weakened the Confederacy. But we still do not know all that much about the women who supported deserters and guerrilla activities, or the women who rioted and mobbed in the fight to feed their families. How did women actually navigate a disparate world in chaos where men had long held mastery? What happened to their mentalities and newfound tools with Emancipation?

We know that the Civil War devastated the physical environment. Its terrible impact ruined crops and destroyed livestock, unleashed diseases, created food deserts, and spoiled water sources.[43] In short, wartime changed entire ecosystems. We have yet to explore the ways wartime attitudes about nature, progress, and the environment were gendered, how social and legal systems of power responded to these new material realities, and how they played out across place, race, and class. We also know that many of our traditional categorizations, and not just the notion of the battlefield, do not hold up that well these days. Much recent work, for example, challenges our once comfortable geographical boundaries of the war and their effect on gender. The reality is that the lines between North and South have gotten increasingly blurred the more we look at them. Consider Washington, D.C., as a case in point, where freedwomen negotiated with federal agencies to find their children and legitimize their marriages. The South as a category itself is also problematic when you think about women's experience of it: in the Missouri borderlands, where no real separation between war front and home front existed; for white and black women in Sherman's path in Georgia; or with white and black women's encounters in Union-occupied Mississippi.

In the introduction to their important collection *Occupied Women* (2009), LeeAnn Whites and Alecia P. Long call for all historians to bring gendered analysis to every aspect of Civil War scholarship. Like Clinton and Silber's *Battle Scars*, the essays in this volume show how the existing classifications of battles and battlefields have largely omitted women. They demand the extension of the traditional definition of the battlefield to include the home front. They insist, as fifty years of great scholarship in this field has made clear, that the Civil War must be reconceptualized as an era, one that stretches from before to after the Civil War, and must no longer be tightly defined by four years of military fighting. The SAWH must continue to support this burgeoning body of work but also press for the inclusion of women's and gender history throughout all Civil War scholarship. May there be many one-volume Civil War histories that truly integrate this scholarship over the course of the SAWH's next fifty years.

Acknowledgments

The author wishes to thank Bill Link, Richard J. Milbauer Professor, for his generous support of this SAWH conference and for his helpful comments on an earlier version of this essay, all the participants in the conference itself, the SAWH, and Catherine Clinton, Denman Professor of American History at the University of Texas at San Antonio, who invited me to participate and whose dazzling contributions to this field inspired me to write this essay in her honor.

Notes

1. For a popular essay conveying the exceptional mettle of Civil War soldiers on the battlefield and across their postwar lifetimes, see Stephen Berry, "When Metal Meets Mettle: The Hard Realities of Civil War Soldiering," *North & South* 9, no. 4: 12–21.

2. Colleen Flaherty, "The Assault on Gender and Gender Studies," *Inside Higher Ed*, November 16, 2018.

3. Paul Escott, *Rethinking the Civil War: Directions for Research* (Lexington: University Press of Kentucky, 2018), ix–xi.

4. Historians' Forum: "*Bonnet Brigades* at 50: Reflections on Mary Elizabeth Massey and Gender in Civil War History" featuring: Judith Giesberg, Nina Silber, Joan Cashin, Thavolia Glymph, Lyde Cullen Sizer, Amy Murrell Taylor, Catherine Clinton, and Eileen Brumitt in *Civil War History* 61, no. 4 (December 2015): 400–429; Panel: "Pioneers and New Scholarship on Women in the Pre-Civil War South," Organization of American Historians Annual Meeting, April 2017.

5. Two outstanding anthologies in particular best convey the profound impact that women's and gender history should be having on interpretations of the Civil War past. See Catherine Clinton and Nina Silber, ed., *Battle Scars: Gender and Sexuality in the American Civil War* (New York: Oxford University Press, 2006), and LeeAnn Whites and Alecia P. Long, ed., *Occupied Women: Gender, Military Occupation, and the American Civil War* (Baton Rouge: Louisiana State University Press, 2009).

6. For an excellent historiographical essay, see Nina Silber's introduction, "Colliding and Collaborating: Gender and Civil War Scholarship," in *Battle Scars*, 3–18.

7. Catherine Clinton and Nina Silber, ed., *Divided Houses: Gender and the Civil War* (New York: Oxford University Press, 1992).

8. Michele Gillespie and Catherine Clinton, ed., *Taking Off the White Gloves: Southern Women and Women Historians* (Columbia: University of Missouri, 1998), 119.

9. Anne Firor Scott, *The Southern Lady: From Pedestal to Politics, 1830–1930* (Chicago: University of Chicago Press, 1970); C. Vann Woodward, ed., *Mary Chesnut's Civil War* (New Haven, Conn.: Yale University Press, 1981).

10. "A Statistical Report on the Participation of Women in the Southern Historical Association, 1935–1985," *Journal of Southern History* 52, no. 2 (May 1986): 286.

11. Carina Chocano, "Conventional Wisdom," *New York Times Sunday Magazine*, October 28, 2018, 11–14.

12. Gillespie and Clinton, ed., *Taking Off the White Gloves*, 147, 152, 153–57. In her 1972 presidential address, Mary Elizabeth Massey pointed out to the nearly all-male audience that female historians received fewer promotions and lower salaries than men. She even recounted her first encounter with her future graduate adviser at UNC. When she told him that she had heard he didn't welcome women, he had replied, "It's not that we don't welcome them. It's just that we don't do anything for them."

13. Colleen Flaherty, "The Impact of Female Chairs," *Inside Higher Ed*, November 14, 2018; Elizabeth J. Allan, ASHE Higher Education Report, "Women's Status in Higher Education: Equity Matters," special issue 37, no. 1 (2011).

14. Catherine Clinton, "The Southern Social Network," *Journal of Southern History* 83, no. 1 (2017): 7–36.

15. LeeAnn Whites, *The Civil War as a Crisis in Gender: Augusta, Georgia, 1860–1890* (Athens: University of Georgia Press, 1995).

16. Drew Gilpin Faust, *Mothers of Invention: Women of the Slaveholding South in the American Civil War* (Chapel Hill: University of North Carolina Press, 1996).

17. See "The Valley of the Shadow" website at http://valley.lib.virginia.edu/.

18. Joan E. Cashin, ed., *The War Was You and Me: Civilians in the American Civil War* (Princeton, N.J.: Princeton University Press, 2002).

19. Amy Murrell Taylor, *The Divided Family in Civil War America* (Chapel Hill: University of North Carolina Press, 2005). See also Victoria E. Ott, *Confederate Daughters: Coming of Age during the Civil War* (Carbondale: Southern Illinois University Press, 2008); and Anya Jabour, *Scarlett's Sisters: Young Women in the Old South* (Chapel Hill: University of North Carolina Press, 2007).

20. Anne Sarah Rubin, *A Shattered Nation: The Rise and Fall of the Confederacy, 1861–1868* (Chapel Hill: University of North Carolina Press, 2005).

21. Anne Marshall, *Creating a Confederate Kentucky: The Lost Cause and Civil War Memory in a Border State* (Chapel Hill: University of North Carolina Press, 2010).

22. See the discussion of the revisions of Civil War mortality. J. David Hacker, "A Census-Based Count of the Civil War Dead," *Civil War History* 57, no. 4 (2011): 307–48. https://muse.jhu.edu/ (accessed September 2, 2019).

23. See also Kim Murphy, *I Had Rather Die: Rape in the Civil War* (Afton, Va.: Coachlight, 2014).

24. Stephanie McCurry, *Confederate Reckoning: Power and Politics in the Civil War South* (Cambridge, Mass.: Harvard University Press, 2010).

25. Jacqueline Glass Campbell, *When Sherman Marched North from the Sea: Resistance on the Confederate Home Front* (Chapel Hill: University of North Carolina Press, 2003). See also Anne Sarah Rubin, *Through the Heart of Dixie: Sherman's March and American Memory* (Chapel Hill: University of North Carolina Press, 2014).

26. Lisa Tendrich Frank, *The Civilian War: Confederate Women and Union Soldiers during Sherman's March* (Baton Rouge: Louisiana State University Press, 2015); see also Stephen Kantrowitz, "Fighting Like Men: Civil War Dilemmas of Abolitionist Manhood," in Clinton and Silber, *Battle Scars*, 19–40.

27. Diane Miller Somerville, "'A Burden Too Heavy to Bear': War Trauma, Suicide, and Confederate Soldiers," *Civil War History* (December 2013). See also Catherine Clinton, "Sex, Insanity and Union Soldiers: The View from St. Elizabeth's Asylum during the Civil War," Society of Civil War Historians Conference, Chattanooga, Tennessee, June 2016.

28. Leslie A. Schwalm, *A Hard Fight for We: Women's Transition from Slavery to Freedom in South Carolina* (Urbana: University of Illinois Press, 1997).

29. Jim Downs, "The Other Side of Freedom: Destitution, Disease, and Dependency among Freedwomen and Their Children during and after the Civil War," in Clinton and Silber, *Battle Scars*, 78–103, and Lisa Cardyn, "Sexual Terror in the Reconstruction South," also in *Battle Scars*, 140–67.

30. Amy Murrell Taylor, *Embattled Freedom: Journeys through the Civil War's Slave Refugee Camps* (Chapel Hill: University of North Carolina Press, 2018). See also Chandra Manning, *Troubled Refuge: Struggling for Freedom in the Civil War* (New York: Knopf, 2016).

31. Crystal Feimster, "'Indecent and Obscene': White Officers, Black Women, and Rape in the 'Contraband Quarters of the American Civil War,'" Southern Association for Women Historians Annual Address at the Southern Historical Association's seventy-eighth Annual Meetings, November 2012.

32. Thavolia Glymph, "'Invisible Disabilities': Black Women in War and in Freedom," Proceedings of the American Philosophical Society 160, no. 3 (September 2016): 237–46.

33. Alice Bolin, *Dead Girls: Essays on Surviving an American Obsession* (New York: HarperCollins, 2018).

34. Judith Giesberg, "Northern Women," in "The Future of Civil War Era Studies" forum, online, *Journal of the Civil War Era Studies*: https://www.journalof thecivilwarera.org/forum-the-future-of-civil-war-era-studies/the-future-of-civil-war-era-studies-northern-women/.

35. Alisha Hines, "Geographies of Freedom: Black Women's Mobility and the Making of the Western River World, 1814–1865," Ph.D. dissertation, Duke University, 2018.

36. Glenda Gilmore, "'But She Can't Find her [V.O.] Key': Writing Gender and Race in Southern Political History," SAWH Address, SHA Annual Meeting, October 1996.

37. Besides the *Divided Houses* and *Battle Scars* collections already cited, Catherine Clin-

ton's pathbreaking Civil War–era works include *Stepdaughters of History: Southern Women and the American Civil War*, Walter Lynwood Fleming Lectures in Southern History (Baton Rouge: Louisiana State University Press, 2016); and, most recently, *Confederate Statues and Memorialization* (Athens: University of Georgia Press, 2019). Her biographies include *Harriet Tubman: The Road to Freedom* (Boston: Little, Brown, 2004); *Mrs. Lincoln: A Life* (New York: Harper, 2009); *Fanny Kemble's Civil Wars* (New York: Simon & Schuster, 2000). Her broader work in the area includes *Tara Revisited: Women, War, and the Plantation Legend* (New York: Abbeville, 1995); and *Civil War Stories*, Jack N. and Addie D. Averitt Lecture Series (Athens: University of Georgia Press, 1998). Her edited volumes include *Mary Chesnut's Diary* (New York: Penguin Classics, reprint ed., 2011); *Fanny Kemble's Journals* (Cambridge, Mass.: Harvard University Press, 2000); "Introduction," *Reminiscences of My Life in Camp: An African American Woman's Civil War Memoir* (Athens: University of Georgia Press, 2006); and the anthology, *Southern Families at War: Loyalty and Conflict in the Civil War South* (New York: Oxford University Press, 2000).

38. Stephanie McCurry, *Women's War: Fighting and Surviving the American Civil War* (Cambridge: Belknap, 2019). Thavolia Glymph's book, *The Women's Fight: The Civil War's Battles for Home, Freedom, and Nation* (Chapel Hill: University of North Carolina, 2020), promises to open up even more debates, as her one-volume analysis of black and white, North and South, has garnered advance praise.

39. Jill Lepore, *These Truths: A History of the United States* (New York: W. W. Norton, 2018).

40. Ashley Whitehead Luskey and Robert M. Dunkerly, "From Women's History to Gender History: Revamping Interpretive Programming at Richmond National Battlefield Park," *Civil War History* 62 (June 2016): 149–69.

41. Escott, *Rethinking the Civil War Era*, 69.

42. Escott, *Rethinking the Civil War Era*, 8–19; Leigh Fought, *Southern Womanhood and Slavery: A Biography of Louisa S. McCord* (Columbia: University of Missouri Press, 2003); Kimberly Harrison, *The Rhetoric of Rebel Women: Civil War Diaries and Confederate Persuasion* (Carbondale: Southern Illinois Press, 2013).

43. See Megan Kate Nelson, *Ruin Nation: Destruction and the American Civil War* (Athens: University of Georgia Press, 2012).

3

A Place Where Women Can Feel Valued, or Why Academic
Professional Associations Matter, Especially for Women

MELISSA WALKER

In 2003, historian Elizabeth Jacoway told an interviewer, "I think that the fact that [the SAWH] is so wildly successful speaks to the need . . . women . . . feel to have a place where they can go . . . and feel that they are valued."[1] As Jacoway suggested, the Southern Association for Women Historians (SAWH) provided a place where female historians felt validated and emboldened. By providing this space over the past five decades, the SAWH has done two important things: advance the careers of individual female historians and encourage, develop, and legitimize the study of women's history. In the process, as several of the scholars here have already suggested, the SAWH helped transform the historiography of the American South by refocusing many of the lenses that scholars have trained on the past. The history of the SAWH demonstrates the crucial role that scholarly professional associations play in shaping fields of knowledge and the careers of individual scholars.

Professionalization and the Emergence of Professional Associations

The history of the SAWH must be understood in the context of the evolving culture of professionalism in the United States and especially the entry of women into the professions. Professionalization is the social process by which people practicing a particular occupation set standards for best practices that differentiate between qualified and unqualified practitioners. Advocates of professionalization sought to develop and advance new forms of knowledge and offer expert services. A major goal of professionalization was to restrict access to specific occupational fields to people who met agreed-upon standards of competence. Proponents of professionalization emphasized that entry to the professions should be controlled by merit and performance, and they asserted that their motivations were altruistic: professionals provided value to the larger society. In the late nineteenth and early twentieth centuries, professional associations became the collective gatekeepers that developed acceptable qualifications for entry into the profession and oversaw the conduct of its members.[2]

Professionalization took root in American law and medicine in the middle decades of the nineteenth century. By the early twentieth century, American universities had also begun to embrace the culture of professionalism. Graduate programs became the entree to college faculty positions. Academics began to pursue professional advancement, often on a national rather than intra-university stage. Though the process could differ a bit from discipline to discipline, academics, like members of the other professions, promoted their national visibility through involvement in professional organizations. Holding leadership roles in these organizations became a major route to professional advancement.[3]

Scholarship from the management literature broadens our understanding of the reasons professional associations were crucial tools for professional advancement. In her pathbreaking 1977 study of gender dynamics in the corporate world, management expert Rosabeth Moss Kanter found that informal professional networks were as essential to individual advancement as formal institutional hierarchies and that sponsors were particularly important. Sponsors are people who wield power in organizations and professions and use that power to advance promising younger professionals by providing them with insider information and advice that advanced their careers. Kanter noted that sponsors were even more essential for women than men because of women's already disadvantaged position in the workforce. Nonetheless, women found it more difficult to find sponsors in male-dominated professions than did their male counterparts. Certainly, stories of how the academic job market worked in the old days, when male graduate advisors picked up the phone and contacted members of their own professional associations to secure jobs—usually unadvertised jobs—for promising male protégés, suggest that sponsorship was just as important in the historical profession as in businesses.[4]

Kanter also noted that strong alliances among peers also help advance careers, sometimes through direct exchange of favors. She concluded, "Power is always accumulated through alliances with sponsors [and] successful peers." Academic professional associations could be fertile ground for cultivating strong networks of sponsors and peers. In academia, perhaps more than most professions, professional associations facilitate job searches and access to grant funding as well as provide publication opportunities, awards, and other validation of one's professional competence that are key to advancement. Indeed, in one of the few studies to look at the keys to advancement in the higher education, Sheila T. Gregory found that access to mentors and to professional networks were key factors in black women's success in the academy.[5]

From their nineteenth-century beginnings, professional associations usually sought to exclude African Americans and women. Black professionals of both sexes faced ostracism and discrimination from white professionals. Denied membership in white professional associations, they founded their own groups. Darlene Clark Hine has shown how black professionals, denied membership in white professional associations, built and nurtured their own organizations, which proved essential to professional success. Hine characterizes the formation of separate black professional associations as a "class-based resistance to racial oppression and exploitation."[6]

Like African Americans, in the late nineteenth century, white professional women began to form single-gender professional associations. Female physicians founded women's medical societies that aimed to publicize the discrimination faced by female doctors, exert pressure on the male medical establishment to include women, inform women of new job opportunities, and tout the professional achievements of female physicians. Women's medical associations often established their own journals in which to publish clinical studies. These organizations offered members a chance to share feedback on each other's papers and subsequently publish them. By the 1890s, female lawyers and women in science had pursued a similar strategy, forming separate scientific associations and publishing their own proceedings. Some professional women objected to the formation of single-gender associations, arguing that organizing separately would only further marginalize them in the professional community, but women's professional associations grew well into the early decades of the twentieth century.[7]

By the early twentieth century, professional associations had emerged as essential institutions in setting and maintaining professional standards in most fields, nurturing new generations of professionals, and shaping the trends in each profession. Particularly in academia, where young professionals competed on a national job market and among national publishing houses and scholarly journals for opportunities, professional associations provided access to the sponsors and mentors essential to advancement. For academic women, lack of access to full participation and leadership roles in professional associations was a major obstacle to career success.

Professionalization and Female Historians

As professionalization took hold in the discipline of history, women who had once found some success and acceptance as published historians found themselves marginalized. For centuries, writing history had been seen as a branch of literature, philosophy, or even theology. In the late nineteenth century, a number of American women had gained prominence as prolific and respected writers of history, including Martha Lamb, publisher of the *Magazine of American History*, Elizabeth Ellet a chronicler of women's contributions to the American Revolution, and Alice Earle, who wrote about the history of women and domestic life. As the scholarly record of these women suggests, some of these early female historians found success by exploring the history of their own sex.[8]

In the late nineteenth century, as the study and writing of history was slowly transformed into a profession requiring advanced degrees and participation in national professional associations, women like Lamb, Ellet, and Earle were marginalized. Even as ever-increasing numbers of middle-class women were attaining college degrees and looking for opportunities to contribute to society beyond home and family, women with aspirations to become respected historians were barred from entrance to many universities, particularly graduate programs, and denied most faculty positions. Even women who did enjoy some success as historians found they could find acceptance only by focusing their scholarly lens on history as made by men, in sharp contrast to women like Elizabeth Ellet, who developed a viable career writing about women's history.[9]

Historians Penina Migdal Glazer and Miriam Slater found that women who earned master's degrees and doctorates often found faculty positions in the growing number of women's colleges. Female academics in single-sex colleges created separate communities for female scholars. Here, Glazer and Slater note, women "found themselves living in a special style of community that fostered an intellectual life and facilitated career aspirations." Although female historians worked to foster the careers of their own students, few had benefited from strong support from male mentors.[10]

Female historians' distinctive gendered experience did not translate to scholarly attention in past women's experiences in the world. In a case study of the Mount Holyoke College History Department, Glazer and Slater found that female historians were well aware of their experience as female scholars operating in a single-gender community, but they never translated this awareness of their distinctive experience into a set of scholarly questions about the past. They resisted any effort to use gender as a category of historical analysis or to examine women's experience as distinctive from men's. Most of the department focused on institutional and constitutional history, the hot field of the day. Their research also focused almost exclusively on male historical actors.[11]

Starting around 1930, a number of factors conspired to diminish the numbers of women pursuing scholarly careers nationwide. In her 1964 study *Academic*

Women, Jesse Bernard called the period from 1930 to 1960 the "great withdrawal." The number of women earning advanced degrees had peaked in 1930. For the next thirty years, the number of women on college and university faculties declined in both raw numbers and in proportion. Women's colleges also faced diminishing status, in part because the research university emerged as the ideal for higher education in the post–World War II period. Since women had never found wide acceptance as faculty members at research universities, they found it difficult to capitalize on the postwar expansion of faculty opportunities there. Financial constraints made it difficult for women's colleges to build doctoral programs that would have boosted their standing to that of research universities, and smaller women's colleges could not attract the ambitious students who came to the elite Seven Sisters. Finally, as the number of women earning Ph.D.s declined, more men became faculty members at the women's colleges. The proportion of female college faculty declined from the 1930s to the late 1950s.[12]

Scholars have suggested a number of reasons for the declining numbers of women in academic professions. Barbara Solomon noted that the persistence of discrimination and the collapse of the feminist movement in the 1920s contributed to the "great withdrawal." Jesse Bernard concluded that this decline resulted from women's shift in preference away from academia toward traditional marriages, homemaking, and childcare. By the late years of the depression, both marriage and birth rates had begun to rise among all women, including college-educated women. The question of how to balance academic careers with marriage and family never really went away and discouraged many young women from following in their faculty members' footsteps.[13]

In addition to these structural and cultural barriers, the challenge of finding mentors who could open doors to professional opportunities was a major obstacle in maintaining the momentum of women's entry into the historical professions. As Glazer and Slater point out, this challenge persisted even among the savvy women in the History Department at Mount Holyoke:

> Seldom were they able to secure their hard won [*sic*] places for future generations. Lacking access to the structures that could facilitate their careers, each generation of women had to start anew. Female neophytes had to be prepared de novo to expend the energy and offer personal sacrifices as if a previous generation of pioneers had not already proven that women could be excellent contributors to the profession. By contrast their male counterparts provided growing opportunities and institutionalized patronage practices for younger men through mentor relationships and informal informational networks as well as through the formal

powers of selection they held on licensing boards, in senior partnerships, and in high administrative posts.[14]

Female historians living and working in the South had similar experiences. In her book *Unheard Voices: The First Historians of Southern Women*, Anne Firor Scott profiles five female historians born in Southern states between 1895 and 1903 who produced pathbreaking work in Southern social history. All five became practicing historians, but "not one achieved a recognized position in the historical profession, and their work lay almost unnoticed for decades." In spite of their distinguished work, none benefited from robust support from male mentors. For example, Virginia Gearhart Gray earned a Ph.D. in 1928 at the University of Wisconsin under the guidance of three well-established male historians who enthusiastically endorsed her for a dissertation fellowship to complete a detailed study of antebellum white women's advocacy of married women's property laws and their work organizing women's voluntary associations. Scott notes, "Given that all three of her mentors were men active and well connected in the discipline one would expect to find that in no very long time she would have been asked to appear on scholarly programs and that her work would speedily have been incorporated in the various surveys of Southern history then being written." This was not the case, however. Scott points out that the work these women pursued, with its focus on women and non-elite populations, "was in a field that male historians simply did not recognize." In *Clio's Southern Sisters*, Scott notes that the male historians who dominated the OAH and the SHA before 1970 "were so sweet, so generous, so Southern gentlemanly, and so impervious. They truly treated individual people with great courtesy and always acted as if you were just absolutely wonderful, but they wouldn't read what you wrote."[15]

Women confronted a similar lack of interest in women's history among editors of scholarly journals. When A. Elizabeth Taylor submitted an article drawn from her dissertation work on the suffrage movement in Tennessee to the *Tennessee Historical Quarterly*, she was told, "We think an article of this type . . . is better suited to the League of Women Voters' publication, or the AAUW [American Association of University Women]." She finally got it published by the *Georgia Historical Quarterly*. She adds, "On programs, the subject [women's history] was always a handicap because I was told, 'We don't have anything to pair yours with.'" Some women resisted studying women's history because, as one said, "'I wouldn't want to be identified with a subject about women. That's just poison.' They just thought I put myself at a disadvantage [by studying women's history]."[16]

Female Historians in the Historical Profession

Because participation in professional associations was a key marker of recognition as legitimate practitioners of a profession, female historians sought to participate in major professional associations. In a study of pioneering professional female historians, Kathryn Kish Sklar found that a few managed to participate at high levels in professional associations. Lucy Salmon (1853–1927), for example, was a founding member of the American Historical Association in 1884. In 1930, Louise Kellogg (1862–1942) was elected president of the Mississippi Valley Historical Association (now the Organization of American Historians). Not until 1946 would the Southern Historical Association elect a woman president, Ella Lonn from Goucher College. Nonetheless Salmon, Lonn, and Kellogg were exceptional; in the first two-thirds of the twentieth century, few women advanced to leadership roles in professional associations, and few were able to publish their work in major historical journals. A further obstacle to women achieving equal status in professional organizations was the context in which much of the organizational business was conducted. Much of the networking at professional meetings took place in all-male gatherings called "smokers" where women were not welcome. Thus women were not included in the informal networks of the profession, which led to sponsorship and peer mentoring that Kanter noted was critical to learning about job opportunities, funding, and publication venues.[17]

Compared to women in other professions, female historians came late to the formation of separate professional associations. In 1930, a group of female historians gathered in Lakeville, Connecticut, and formed a group they called the Lakeville History Group. It was founded to promote their interests, and it welcomed women from all historical specialties. In 1935, the organization was renamed the Berkshire Conference of Women Historians (to reflect its meeting place in the Berkshire mountains). For many years, the Berkshire Conference remained a small group of historians primarily from the Northeast who gathered annually for networking and support. Not until 1968, in the wake of second-wave feminism, did the organization begin to offer book prizes for outstanding scholarship by women. In 1973, it held its first conference on women's history, and at that point the organization began shifting to the focus on women's and gender studies that it maintains to this day.[18]

As the history of the Berkshire Conference suggests, it would take the great social ferment that engulfed the nation in the 1960s and 1970s to launch a grassroots movement for women's equality within the historical profession. Women's involvement in the grassroots organizing of the civil rights movement helped spark a new feminist consciousness and a second wave of the women's rights movement. This new women's movement was dominated by middle-class women who aspired to professional careers. A number of legal milestones, including the Equal Pay Act of 1963 (expanded in 1972 to cover professional and administrative employees), fueled demands for equal pay for equal work. Title VII of the Civil Rights Act of 1964 opened the door to eliminating sex discrimination in employment via the legal system, and Title IX's prohibition on sex discrimination in any educational program that received federal funding began to broaden women's opportunities for graduate and professional education. The formation of women's rights groups such as the National Organization for Women and the Women's Equity Action League as well as women's activism in the civil rights movement meant that many in the new generation of historians had experience with grassroots activism. Activists focused on consciousness-raising, which increased awareness of the social and structural obstacles to women's achievement, unleashing a wave of women's discontent with the status quo. And finally, the youth movements of the era gave rise to demands from college students to broaden both the structures and the content of the curriculum to include black and ethnic studies and women's studies, which would in turn fuel a demand for a more inclusive curriculum and faculty in history departments.[19]

In the wake of all this social and cultural ferment and change, young female historians had strong ambitions but still found their opportunities limited. By the early 1970s, women were pursuing Ph.D.s in numbers not seen since the 1920s, but women who earned doctorates were frustrated because the structure of professional life still disadvantaged them. Female historians found that they could interact with men in professional associations but that they rarely ascended to leadership positions, and they were segregated into their own track of jobs, outside coed or male institutions. In short, they continued to face overwhelming obstacles to competing with men on the job market.[20]

In oral history interviews and autobiographical essays, a number of the early leaders of the SAWH reflected on the obstacles facing female historians who entered the profession in the 1960s and 1970s. Margaret Ripley Wolfe recalls, "It would never have occurred to any of the men I dealt with at . . . [her graduate program at University of Kentucky and her department at ETSU] to encourage me to attend a professional meeting." Arnita Jones describes calling the placement office at Emory about ten years after she finished her doctorate and learning about the contents of the recommendations in her placement file: "They were letters by these men at Emory; trying, because they thought I was a good student and they liked me, to do the best they could for me. One comment I remember was something like, 'Miss Ament seems really quite normal, and I think would fit in easily.' I mean literally stuff like that. . . . And I wanted to cry after I listened because these guys were trying to help me. . . . A lot of language about appearance, a lot. I mean I don't think there was a letter that didn't describe how I looked."

Mollie C. Davis says, "I think women in particular weren't taught by their mentors or anyone how to make a contract, . . . and everything [in the profession] was so secret."[21]

In this context, women turned to each other for support, first at the national level. Frustrated that the American Historical Association seemed committed to preserving the dominance of white male historians in the profession, a group of women at the 1969 AHA meeting came together to form the Coordinating Committee on Women in the Historical Profession. CCWHP was formed "to encourage the recruitment of women into the historical profession, to oppose discrimination against women in the profession, and to encourage research and instruction in women's history." In the introduction to their collection of autobiographical essays by CCWHP founders, Eileen Boris and Nupur Chaudhuri note that the CCWHP emerged "out of the activist ferment that marked a new cohort of women in the profession who turned their scholarly gaze toward the recovery of women's experiences." Mollie Davis, who would later become a founding member of the SAWH, was a founding officer of CCWHP while she was still a graduate student. A grassroots activist all her life, she brought an activist sensibility to her work as a historian. Davis recalled that through the CCWHP, female historians advocated for each other's appointment to professional association committees: "CCWHP and its sisterly network helped open up positions for many of us, including me. . . . I am fairly certain that CCWHP advocates promoted my appointment to the Organization of American Historians' Committee on Women."[22]

Female historians were also frustrated with their marginalization in the Southern Historical Association. As Constance Schulz and Elizabeth Hayes Turner note in the introduction to *Clio's Southern Sisters*, "Before 1970, women historians in the South could turn to few role models for professional guidance within the Southern Historical Association." In 1970, thirty of these frustrated female historians, including Mollie Davis, came together at the annual meeting of the Southern Historical Association in Louisville, Kentucky, to form a loose coalition called the Caucus of Women Historians. One of the women present in Louisville, Barbara Brandon Schnorrenberg, summed up the twin goals of the founding members: "to encourage interest and panels and programs on women's history . . . to get more women onto committees and power positions of the SHA."[23]

The loosely organized Caucus of Women Historians grew over the next decade and a half, and by 1985, they had renamed themselves the Southern Association for Women Historians and opened membership to all historians, male and female, inside and outside the South, who supported its mission of advancing women in the historical profession and promoting the study of Southern women's history. The first phase of the SAWH, between 1970 and 1975, was concentrated on developing lines of communication and mutual support among Southern female historians and on raising the consciousness of the profession through documentation of the status and participation of Southern female historians in teaching, publishing, presenting papers at conferences, and serving on committees.[24] One early SAWH leader, Betty Brandon, said in the early days, the SAWH was a "mechanism for information, for support, for conversation."[25]

As the SAWH grew from an informal "caucus" of women working within the SHA to a well-organized body offering a broad range of member services, the organization's leaders not only sought to advance the careers of its members but also took important steps to encourage and validate the study of women's history. For example, most historical organizations celebrated the induction of a new president by having that scholar present an annual address to the membership, but the SAWH took a different approach. Each SAWH president asked a leading scholar of women's history to give an annual lecture, thus institutionalizing the idea of professional female historians advancing the careers of other female historians. The lectures also helped promote acceptance of the study of Southern women's history, because they were held at the SHA annual meeting and all SHA attendees were invited. Indeed, everyone attending the SHA was invited to attend the lecture and the gala reception that followed. From the first annual address, offered by A. Elizabeth Taylor at the 1979 SHA meeting in Atlanta, the SAWH lecture and reception became a highlight of the meeting. In fact, members often commented that the SAWH had a reputation for giving the best parties at the Southern.[26]

The organization also used book prizes to both advance the careers of female scholars and encourage the study of Southern women's history. In the late 1980s, the SAWH raised funds to establish two book prizes: the Julia Cherry Spruill Prize, for the best book in Southern women's history, and the Willie Lee Rose Prize, for the best book in Southern history authored by a woman. (Later the organization added the A. Elizabeth Taylor Prize, for the best article on Southern women's history, and the Jacquelyn Dowd Hall Prize, for the best papers presented by graduate students at the triennial conference.) By presenting these prizes at the annual address, the organization again increased the visibility of outstanding scholarship on women's history.[27]

Seeking to further expand opportunities for scholars studying women's history to share their work and exchange ideas, and inspired, in part, by the example of the successful Berkshire conference, the SAWH organized the first Southern Conference on Women's History. The event, held at Converse College in Spartanburg, South Carolina, in June 1988, attracted nearly four hundred people, including a few men. The event also coincided with Converse's centennial year. The conference provoked lively conversations about historiography, research, and the challenges of studying and writing women's history. It led to a series of triennial conferences.[28]

Professional associations are in many ways, microcosms of the larger society, and they are sometimes rent by the same tensions present in that society. Upon occasion, conflicts over race have emerged in the SAWH, and this happened at the first conference. Black female historians had long faced discrimination within the academy. Even in the earliest days of professionalization, they were not welcomed on the faculty of white institutions, and they were not welcomed by their female peers at the Berkshire Conference of Women Historians. To make matters worse, as historian Deborah Gray White observes, "For black women historians, the black scholarly world proved almost as difficult to enter as the white. Black male scholars were just as engaged as their white counterparts in the project of masculinizing history by associating themselves with scientific methodology and objectivity," and they resisted women's efforts to "place women at the center of black history." For decades, women were not included in the major organizations of African American historians or published in the *Journal of Negro History*. The earliest black female historians had few people with whom to share experiences and few role models. Rosalyn Terborg-Penn recalls that in the late 1970s, she was involved in the Association for the Study of African American Life and History, where the prevailing attitude among many of the black men who attended conferences was sexist. Many of them argued that women's history was feminism and that it distracted from the struggle to legitimize black studies. Several of my black female colleagues have noted this phenomenon—racism from white feminist scholars and sexism from black nationalist male scholars.

For many of these women, the formula for survival was simply to be more qualified than men and to outlast them. But for others, including Eleanor Smith, Elizabeth Parker, and Rosalyn Terborg-Penn, the solution was to create a nationwide organization for black female historians, the Association of Black Women Historians. Darlene Clark Hine recalls, "The need for a network of mentors was one of the impetuses for the creation of the Association of Black Women Historians."[29]

The SAWH aimed to be inclusive of black female historians and welcomed them into membership and onto the program of the first Southern Conference on Women's History, but the organization was not immune to unconscious biases and institutional racism. Elsa Barkley Brown served on the program committee for the first SAWH conference at Converse in 1988, and she recalls that organizers had worked hard to make sure that the conference was an inclusive of historians of color, grad students, and a wide range of women's histories. Yet, tensions emerged from the first day of the conference. In an early session, a group of white women presented on black women's history and a black female historian was the commentator. The white women bristled at some of the commentary offered by the black female historian. Brown notes, "White women, even many whose own work is deeply engaged with the history of black women, [were] for the first time having to accept black women themselves as historical authorities—not only on black women's history but also, and perhaps more difficult to accept, on women's history in general." Brown adds, "I tell this story not as a critique of the SAWH or any of its members but as a comment on the setting in which we found ourselves—one that was managing to be more inclusive than most other sites within the history wing of the academy and at the same time struggling with what it would really mean to include new histories and recognize new people as historians."[30]

In spite of these tensions, many scholars found the first conference to be career changing. Elizabeth Hayes Turner recalls that she attended that conference when she was a graduate student at Rice University. The conference enabled her to meet several scholars whose work was shaping her own study of female activists in Galveston, including Jacquelyn Dowd Hall and Catherine Clinton. She roomed with another graduate student, Judith McArthur, who was working on a statewide history of Texas female activists. Turner describes the conference as a

> glorious . . . meeting of . . . historians discovering the complexities of Southern women's history. I really thought that this association was an intellectual home, a stimulus for further work, and an organization that fostered and encouraged students. It was there that I met Connie Schulz and later collaborated on *Clio's Southern Sisters*, thanks to the urging of Michele Gillespie. Connie brought her violin and, in the evenings, would pull it out on the dorm steps and play. I may be exaggerating, but it seems that Connie's violin brought out the fireflies—if not, then my memories embroider them there. The first conference and subsequent conferences offered opportunities to meet the well-established women's historians such as Anne Scott, Suzanne Lebsock, Roslyn Terborg-Penn, Darlene Clark Hine, and Jackie Hall. . . . The initial conference provided the opportunity to meet young

scholars and students with similar projects who spoke with enthusiasm about women's history and about their findings. . . . I left that first meeting with euphoria and with the notion that a group of like-minded scholars had found one another. It was indeed life changing.[31]

Informal conversations at the first conference highlighted the fact that women's history scholars struggled to find publication opportunities, so SAWH leaders decided to collect, edit, and publish the best papers from the conference, and they negotiated with the University of Missouri Press to publish an ongoing Southern Women series, which eventually included nine volumes. In 1995, historian Betty Brandon explained that opportunities created by the SAWH to present and publish research on Southern women's history had "ripple effects." She says, "[When] there is some interest and the activities encourage and promote that interest, . . . that just gives opportunities all over the place."[32]

The first Southern Conference on Women's History generated additional momentum. By 1990, SAWH membership had grown to more than four hundred. As the organization expanded, the SAWH leadership poured considerable energy into nurturing grad students by including a graduate representative on its executive council and offering graduate students deeply discounted memberships and conference registration fees. SAWH leaders intentionally developed mentoring opportunities for graduate students and junior scholars by organizing workshops and networking events for graduate students at the SHA and at the triennial meetings. In the early decades of the new millennium, the executive council created formal mechanisms to pair senior scholar mentors with junior scholars seeking advice and support at the SHA and at the triennial meeting. The organization also developed a mentoring toolkit, an online collection of advice on topics including selecting a graduate school, navigating the job search, grants and fellowships, and minority faculty issues. A research fellowship for mid-career scholars was added.[33]

SAWH members were sponsors, as Kanter describes, introducing their own graduate students to the organization by offering them gift memberships and taking them to conferences. Historian Karen L. Cox recalls that her advisor, Marjorie Spruill, gave her a gift membership and took a group of graduate students to the third triennial conference at Rice University in 1994. Cox says, "It was there that I gave my first paper at a scholarly conference and where she introduced me to other scholars. . . . In fact, I think it is at the triennial conference of SAWH where the mentoring of younger scholars is on full display. Workshops, introductions, [and] speakers all give a young scholar a sense of the profession she is entering. And to be able to have a meal or a glass of wine with a more established scholar and talk about the profession in such a relaxed way extends the mentoring that happens at SAWH."[34]

Rebecca Sharpless was another scholar who found that the triennial conference was an essential vehicle for nurturing young scholars. She explains that she attended her first SAWH in 1991: "I was still two years away from finishing my PhD, but the program committee invited me to be on a plenary panel with several senior scholars. I was absolutely awestruck that they would do that. And I took the assignment seriously, being a terrified graduate student, and the senior scholars did not. I remember Linda Schott, who is now president of Southern Oregon U, hugging me and saying mine was the best presentation."[35]

Graduate students also found a supportive network among SAWH at the SHA. Angela Boswell says:

I . . . want to stress the importance of the organization at providing role models. I was in a program with an incredibly supportive advisor who encouraged and nurtured my research on women's topics. But he was a man, as were most of the faculty in the department. The few women in the department studied other parts of the world and had, understandably, little time for this Americanist. As a result, my first year, I had a little trouble imagining myself as a historian. . . . The SAWH, however, gave me a host of women with whom to network, share interests in the discipline, and most importantly, to see as active, successful historians. I doubt I would have made it through the PhD program without those examples. Without the organization, I would have attended the SHA, but the smaller number of women among the large sea of men would have been lost to me. With the organization, at SAWH business meetings, at annual addresses, and at the triennial conferences, I could see what I might become.[36]

Lorri Glover notes that she joined the SAWH as a graduate student:

The leaders of the organization took my work seriously when I was struggling to think of myself as an historian rather than a student. SAWH at SHA was the place I felt most comfortable randomly introducing myself to people and the SAWH conferences became my first professional home. . . . I quickly came to see that the culture was inclusive and gracious. I was encouraged to volunteer, and my volunteering was taken seriously, too. . . . To me, the formal organizational matters—the committee, the breakfasts at SHA, the working groups at our triennial conferences—are manifestations of the deeper cultural tradition of women working for and with women for the good of our profession.[37]

The SAWH welcomed supportive men into its ranks, and some of these men became supporters of female historians. Elizabeth Hayes Turner recalls that she learned about the SAWH from founder Mollie Davis. In turn, Turner brought another important figure into the organization. She explains, "When I entered graduate school at Rice in 1982, I introduced the SAWH to John Boles, who quickly became a member." Through his involvement in the SAWH, the editor of the *Journal of Southern History* became acquainted with the burgeoning field of Southern women's history. In future years, the work of many SAWH members would find a home in the pages of the *JSH*.[38]

Mentoring graduate students was important, but it was not the only form of mentoring that went on among SAWH members. As Harvard management professor Rosabeth Moss Kanter notes, peer-to-peer relationships are essential for women's advancements, and SAWH members repeatedly cite peer mentoring as another benefit of SAWH membership. Historian Cindy Kierner notes, "The friendliness of SAWH to younger scholars made a decisive difference [in my career]. . . . My most important personal and professional connections are primarily with fellow SAWH-ers. The organization has made a huge contribution to my career, and I hope I've repaid the favor."[39]

Karen Cox concurs on the importance of peer mentoring and notes that it often came as a natural outgrowth of peer relationships forged among graduate students at SAWH graduate student events. She says, "Those individuals I met at [my first conference at] Rice University . . . are still friends who I seek out whenever I attend SHA or SAWH. Over the years they've provided a sounding board about writing, publishing, etc., as I have to them." Like Kierner, she seeks to pay forward the benefits of membership to the next generation of scholars:

> That mentoring has borne fruit, because now I am in the position of mentoring junior scholars, which I not only consider an important part of what I do, I enjoy it!! When called upon by graduate students or the organization to be part of a mentoring session, I make every effort to do so, because I know what a benefit it was to me. I also think that now, in the age of social media, those graduate students know this about me and seek me out. I have numerous graduate students following me on Twitter and I them. I give full credit to SAWH for shaping that part of my scholarly life.[40]

As the foregoing examples suggest, the SAWH played a crucial role in advancing women in the profession by nurturing young scholars and peers alike and by mobilizing an "old girls' network" to help women access opportunities within the historical profession. Arnita A. Jones recognized early on "that other women could be a good support group. . . . It was in those organizations that I began to find a network and to realize the possibilities of making some differences."[41] Darlene Clark Hine also credits the SAWH as being the organization where she built mutually supportive relationships with other scholars.[42] Elizabeth Jacoway says that the SAWH was "a very important vehicle for me . . . to stay visible [as an independent scholar.]"[43]

Hine saw another role of the SAWH as "provid[ing] skill training. I'm talking about leadership skills, exposure to ease the path into the larger organizational structure. Also, being an organized body, we are able to identify those women with talents and suggest them to nominating committees and other positions . . . [such as] book prize committees so that they can become more integrally involved in the Southern." Indeed, hundreds of women who honed their leadership skills in the SAWH have gone on to serve the SHA on committees and as officers, including past presidents Carol Bleser, Darlene Clark Hine, Catherine Clinton, Theda Perdue, and Jane Turner Censer.[44]

The work of feminist scholars in organizations like the SAWH would begin to change the attitude that women's history was somehow apart from and less than other historical specialties. Writing in a 1992 historiographical essay that opened the first volume of SAWH conference papers, Jacquelyn Dowd Hall expresses the need for "a historical practice that turns on partiality, that is self-conscious about perspective, that releases multiple voices rather than competing orthodoxies, and that above all, nurtures 'an internally differing but united political community.'" She asserts that only a community of feminist scholars could achieve that kind of historical practice.[45] The SAWH provided one of those communities of feminist scholars.

Nancy Hewitt notes the importance of scholarly networks in shaping her research questions:

> To build connections to historian with similar interests, I depended on networks created by earlier feminist scholars. . . . My service to CCWHP/CCWH assured that the forms of community activism I uncovered while researching immigrant women in Tampa would be in continuous conversation with the regional and global efforts analyzed by an array of feminist academics. The Southern Association of Women Historians (SAWH) [sic] provided a similar network of US historians whose work on race, gender, and class inspired me to expand the Tampa study to include the stories of Anglo and African-American as well as Latin women activists.[46]

Stephanie Cole explored the ways that the work of SAWH members had helped transform understandings of not only Southern history but also U.S. history as a whole. Their work showed how attention to matters of gender complicated notions of progress and challenged the idea of a monolithic category of Southern women, or even Southern white women. Their scholarship highlighted the importance of individual agency and uncovered the idea of overlapping identities, a notion we now call "intersectionality." They have shown how gender ideology can be used to divide or unite various groups of people.[47] Similarly, Darlene Clark Hine notes that the work of black female historians had forced historians in many fields to ask new questions, employ new methods of research and analysis, and to create new conceptual categories.[48]

Over the almost fifty years of its existence, the SAWH has provided a place where, as Elizabeth Jacoway describes, "women could feel that they are valued." The organization provided female historians with opportunities to hone leadership skills, exchange scholarly ideas, interact with role models, and develop supportive peer networks. By skillfully negotiating relationships with the male historians who dominated the Southern Historical Association, SAWH leaders opened doors for female scholars and cultivated scholarly acceptance of the use of gender as a category of analysis. In the process, they have enriched and broadened our understandings of our shared pasts. The example of the SAWH demonstrates that professional associations are essential vehicles for advancement in the academic professions, particularly for women.

Notes

1. Constance B. Schulz and Elizabeth Hayes Turner, eds., *Clio's Southern Sisters: Interviews with Leaders of the Southern Association for Women Historians* (Columbia: University of Missouri Press, 2004), 167.

2. Burton J. Bledstein, *The Culture of Professionalism: The Middle Class and the Development of Higher Education in America* (New York: W. W. Norton, 1976), 319.

3. Penina Migdal Glazer and Miriam Slater, *Unequal Colleagues: The Entrance of Women into the Professions* (New Brunswick: Rutgers University Press, 1987), 2–3. Glazer and Slater offer a case study of the History Department at Mount Holyoke. After Mary Wooley became president of Mt. Holyoke in 1901, she focused on building a faculty that met the highest standards of scholarly excellence. Under her leadership, Mount Holyoke became a community of women scholars. Wooley insisted that all of her faculty have graduate education, and the college offered paid sabbaticals so that faculty could attain doctorates. The college freed its female faculty from all domestic responsibilities by providing housing and meal service. In return, "they enjoyed access to a community of scholars who served as both friends and a reference group for ambitious professionals who were bucking the tide of society" (34). Mount Holyoke did have a handful of male faculty who found themselves shoved to the margins of faculty leadership. The history department at Mount Holyoke was also committed to creating a new generation of female scholars and encouraged their students to go to graduate school. Many of them entered academic life at small teaching colleges. Glazer and Slater, *Unequal Colleagues*, 27–52, 50.

4. Rosabeth Moss Kanter, *Men and Women of the Corporation* (New York: Basic, 1993), 181–84.

5. Kanter, *Men and Women of the Corporation*, 275–76; Sheila T. Gregory, "Black Faculty Women in the Academy: History, Status, and Future," *Journal of Negro Education* 70 (Summer 2001): 131–32.

6. Darlene Clark Hine, *Truth to Power: Black Professional Class in United States History* (Brooklyn: Carlson, 1996): xiv–xxii.

7. Regina Morantz-Sanchez, *Sympathy and Science: Women Physicians in American Medicine* (Chapel Hill: University of North Carolina Press, 2000), 233, 267–68; Margaret W. Rossiter, *Women Scientists in America: Struggles and Strategies to 1940* (Baltimore: Johns Hopkins University Press, 1982), 94–95; Virginia G. Drachman, *Sisters in Law: Women Lawyers in Modern American History* (Cambridge, Mass.: Harvard University Press, 1998), 234–37. Anne Firor Scott has also noted the importance of the Association of Collegiate Alumnae in helping college-educated women, particularly those who pursued professional careers, including academic ones, connect with networks of like-minded women. See Scott, "Making the Invisible Women Visible: An Essay Review," *Journal of Southern History* 38, no. 4 (1972): 635.

8. Kathryn Kish Sklar, "American Female Historians in Context, 1770–1930," *Feminist Studies* 3 (Autumn 1975): 176–78;

9. Theodore S. Hamerow, "The Professionalization of Historical Learning," *Reviews in American History* 14, no. 3 (1986): 319–21; Glazer and Slater, *Unequal Colleagues*, 4, 12–13, 77, 82. Among the general social attitudes that were obstacles to women's entry into all professions, academic and otherwise, was the belief that ambition or leadership aspirations in women were unnatural and unfeminine, that women's appropriate role in society was in creating a home and nurturing a family.

10. Glazer and Slater, *Unequal Colleagues*, 14–15, 27 (quotation); Sklar, "American Female Historians in Context, 1770–1930," 180. In spite of the obstacles, some women did enter the academic professions. In the first four decades of the twentieth century, women were earning between 10 and 15 percent of the annual Ph.D.s in the United States, but faculty positions were few and far between. Historian Barbara Solomon has noted that by 1930, women held 33 percent of graduate degrees but only 4 percent of full professorships in all fields. Barbara Miller Solomon, *In the Company of Educated Women: A History of Women and Higher Education in America* (New Haven: Yale University Press, 1985), 133.

11. Glazer and Slater, *Unequal Colleagues*, 25, 27, 52–53.

12. Barbara J. Harris, *Beyond Her Sphere: Women and the Professions in American History* (Westport, Conn.: Greenwood, 1978), 138; Susan B. Carter, "Academic Women Revisited: An Empirical Study of Changing Patterns in Women's Employment as College and University Faculty, 1890–1963," *Journal of Social History* 14 (Summer 1981): 676–77; Patricia A. Graham, "Expansion and Exclusion: A History of Women in American Higher Education," *Signs: Journal of Women in Culture and Society* 3 (Summer 1978):759–73; Glazer and Slater, *Unequal Colleagues*, 56–57, 25; Harris, *Beyond Her Sphere*, 142. Historian Susan Carter argues that occupational segregation indeed persisted in higher education, with women clustered in "women's fields," but that the mix of types of institutions actually increased after World War II and that this led to an increase in employment of female faculty, albeit in gender-segregated fields. She does not look specifically at disciplines, however, and since history had never been a "woman's field," it is unlikely that opportunities for female historians increased in this period. See Carter, "Academic Women Revisited," 688–90. The trend in academia mir-

rored the trend in other professions. In the 1920s, movement of women into the professions slowed down and in medicine actually reversed itself. The situation reversed during World War II, but it mostly was a temporary reversal. There were more opportunities for female doctors. Harris, *Beyond Her Sphere*, 144.

13. Bernard, cited in Carter, "Academic Women Revisited," 676; Harris, *Beyond Her Sphere*, 144; Glazer and Slater, *Unequal Colleagues*, 62–64.

14. Glazer and Slater, *Unequal Colleagues*, 231–32. Margaret Rossiter notes a similar pattern in the academic sciences. Although the earliest female professors in the sciences became advocates for their students, often training students to be their successors on the faculty of women's colleges, this mentoring did not necessarily translate into opportunities in other types of institutions. Rossiter, *Women Scientists in America*, 18.

15. Anne Firor Scott, *Unheard Voices: The First Historians of Southern Women* (Charlottesville: University of Virginia Press, 1993): 5–16, quotes on 54, 13, 58; Scott in *Clio's Southern Sisters*, 44.

16. A. Elizabeth Taylor in *Clio's Southern Sisters*, 24–25, quote on 24.

17. Sklar, "American Female Historians in Context, 1770–1930," 179; Carol Bleser, ed., "The Three Women Presidents of the Southern Historical Association: Ella Lonn, Kathryn Abby [*sic*] Hanna, and Mary Elizabeth Massey," *Southern Studies* (Summer 1981): 101; History, Berkshire Conference of Women Historians, accessed August 30, 2018 at: https://berksconference.org/about/history/.

18. Sklar, "American Female Historians in Context, 1770–1930," 181–82; "History," Berkshire Conference of Women Historians, accessed September 4, 2018: https://berksconference.org/about/history/.

19. Barbara Solomon shows how the revival of idealized notions of female domesticity in the post–World War II period retarded women's higher education and their entry into the professions (chapter 11) and how the increasing radicalization of young people in the 1960s helped propel women back into the professions (chapter 12). See Barbara Miller Solomon, *In the Company of Educated Women: A History of Women and Higher Education in America* (New Haven: Yale University Press, 1985).

20. Solomon, *In the Company of Educated Women*, 133; Sklar, "American Female Historians in Context, 1770–1930," 182.

21. Wolfe, in Constance B. Schulz and Elizabeth Hayes Turner, eds., *Clio's Southern Sisters: Interviews with Leaders of the Southern Association for Women Historians* (Columbia: University of Missouri Press, 2004), 203; Jones in *Clio's Southern Sisters*, 78; Davis in *Clio's Southern Sisters*, 66.

22. Eileen Boris and Nupur Chaudhuri, eds., *Voices of Women Historians: The Personal, The Political, The Professional* (Bloomington: Indiana University Press, 1999), xi–xiv, quote on xi; and Mollie C. Davis, "Two Catalysts in My Life: Voter Registration Drives and CCWHP," 135–43.

23. Schulz and Turner, *Clio's Southern Sisters*, introduction, *Clio's Southern Sisters*, 19, 8–10. For more on the dearth of female role models in the Southern historical profession and on those first three women to serve as president of the SHA, see Carol K. Bleser, "Tokens of Affection: The First Three Women Presidents of the Southern Historical Association," in *Taking Off the White Gloves: Southern Women and Women Historians*, ed. Michele Gillespie and Catherine Clinton, 145–57 (Columbia: University of Missouri, 1998); and Carol K. Bleser,

"The Three Women Presidents of the Southern Historical Association, Ella Lonn, Kathryn Abby [sic] Hanna, and Mary Elizabeth Massey," *Southern Studies* (Summer 1981): 101–21.

24. Schulz and Turner, introduction, *Clio's Southern Sisters,* 10–12; Schnorrenberg, in *Clio's Southern Sisters,* 57–58.

25. Brandon in *Clio's Southern Sisters,* 196.

26. Schulz and Turner, introduction, *Clio's Southern Sisters,* 11.

27. Schulz and Turner, introduction, *Clio's Southern Sisters,* 11.

28. Schulz and Turner, introduction, *Clio's Southern Sisters,* 13–14. In 2018, the eleventh triennial conference met at the University of Alabama.

29. White, "Introduction: A Telling History," in *Telling Histories: Black Women Historians in the Ivory* Tower, ed. Deborah Gray White (Chapel Hill: University of North Carolina Press, 2008), 12, 19–20; Rosalyn Terborg-Penn, "Being and Thinking Outside the Box: A Black Woman's Experience in Academia," in *Telling Histories,* 79–80; Darlene Clark Hine, "Becoming a Black Woman's Historian," in *Telling Histories,* 53–54.

30. Elsa Barkley Brown, "Bodies of History," in *Telling Histories,* 215–16.

31. Elizabeth Hayes Turner, email communication with author, August 22, 2018.

32. Betty Brandon, quoted in *Clio's Southern Sisters,* 192.

33. Schulz and Turner, introduction, *Clio's Southern Sisters,* 13; see also Elizabeth Jacoway, *Clio's Southern Sisters,* 165.

34. Karen Cox, email communication with author, May 28, 2018.

35. Rebecca Sharpless, email communication with author, May 27, 2018.

36. Angela Boswell, email communication with author, July 3, 2018.

37. Lorri Glover, email communication with author, June 4, 2018.

38. Elizabeth Hayes Turner, email communication with author, August 22, 2018.

39. Cynthia Kierner, email communication with author, May 29, 2018.

40. Karen Cox, email communication with author, May 28, 2018.

41. Arnita Jones, in *Clio's Southern Sisters,* 82.

42. Darlene Clark Hine, *Truth to Power: Black Professional Class in United States History* (Brooklyn: Carlson, 1996), 27, 28.

43. Elizabeth Jacoway, in *Clio's Southern Sisters,* 161.

44. Darlene Clark Hine, in *Clio's Southern Sisters,* 223.

45. Jacquelyn Dowd Hall, "Partial Truths: Writing Southern Women's History," in *Southern Women: Histories and Identities,* ed. Virginia Bernhard, Betty Brandon, Elizabeth Fox-Genovese, and Theda Perdue (Columbia: University of Missouri Press, 1992), 28–29.

46. Nancy Hewitt, "The Emma Thread: Communitarian Values, Global Visions," in Boris and Chaudhuri, *Voices of Women Historians,* 244.

47. Stephanie Cole, "Introduction," in *Searching for Their Places: Women in the South Across Four Centuries,* ed. Thomas H. Appleton and Angela Boswell (Columbia: University of Missouri, 2003), 2–3.

48. Darlene Clark Hine, *Truth to Power: Black Professional Class in United States History* (Brooklyn: Carlson, 1996), 55.

4

"Can the Sistas Get Some History, Too?"

Transformations in Southern Black Women's History

CHERISSE JONES-BRANCH

I am a Southern black woman. I was born and raised in Charleston, South Carolina.[1] I am a descendent of the Gullah people. Both the maternal and paternal sides of my family have been in the South Carolina low country since at least the late eighteenth century. I can trace my lineage to former plantations such as Brookgreen Gardens in Murrells Inlet, South Carolina, where my ancestors labored and where, I was once told, some of my relatives lived until as late as the early 1960s. I am the direct descendant of the black women who bore, nursed, raised, and buried all who resided there. We are Southern black women whose lives and stories have not been told in ways that fully acknowledge them as the guiding force in African Americans' ongoing struggle for freedom and liberty. The scholarship on Southern women's history has increased over the past fifty years to be sure, but the remaining silences surrounding black women's existence across time and space still beg the question, "Can the sistas get some history, too?"

I became particularly interested in Southern black women's history while I was a graduate student at the College of Charleston in South Carolina. Actually, let me back up a bit. My first realization of the importance of Southern black women's history came when I was a debutante in 1989. For well over fifty years by that point, Alpha Kappa Alpha Sorority Incorporated (AKA), easily the most elite black women's sorority in Charleston, had sponsored an annual debutante ball. I viewed it as a heinous and bourgeois experience, but my mother, who is an AKA, made me do it. I spent just about every Saturday of my senior year of high school with older members of this organization at their sorority house in downtown Charleston learning how to become a cultured, well-spoken young woman. As irritated as I was by the entire debacle (and by the way, although I am an AKA legacy, I pledged a completely different sorority), as an eighteen-year-old I was nonetheless struck by the organization's history and that of the black women who made up its membership.[2]

Fast-forward to a couple of years later. I had returned from the Persian Gulf War (yes, I am a war veteran) and transferred from South Carolina State University in Orangeburg to the College of Charleston. I am sure that Dr. Amy McCandless, my undergraduate advisor, must have mentioned the Southern Association for Women Historians (SAWH) to me, but I was too busy battling post-traumatic stress disorder to appreciate her words.

I really learned about the SAWH as a graduate student at the College of Charleston. My first encounter with the SAWH was in the 1990s at the College of Charleston. It was there that I first met Catherine Clinton. At the time, I was working on or had completed my master's thesis on Charleston's black club women. She urged me to interview some of the club women I discussed, which I subsequently did. In the process, I learned that cultivating and utilizing community connections was key to unearthing Southern black women's stories because they most often cannot be found in traditional archives. I did not really appreciate the skill necessary to effectively mine marginalized resources then, but I certainly have learned to since then. It has indeed continued to deeply inform my foray into Southern black women's history. The SAWH was a vital connecting force for me in my early career.

To be clear, the ways in which Southern women's history has developed over the past half century have been nothing short of exciting. But in my estimation, the most significant and exciting change within the field has been the ever-increasing production of scholarship on Southern black women's history. From the time I read Deborah Gray White's *Ar'n't I a Woman: Female Slaves in the Plantation South*, Tera Hunter's *To 'Joy My Freedom: Southern Black Women's Lives and Labors after the Civil War*, Stephanie Shaw's *What a Woman Ought to Be and to Do: Black Professional Workers during the Jim Crow Era* (by the way, she was also on my dissertation committee), Paula Giddings's *When and Where I Enter: The Impact of Black Women on Race and Sex in America*, and Darlene Clark Hine's *Hine Sight: Black Women and the Reconstruction of American History*, as well as the scholarship of Thavolia Glymph, in graduate school, I was intrigued by the unearthing and excavation of black women's stories from the caverns of American, African American, Southern, and women's history.[3] This scholarship opened a new, yet entirely familiar world of historical inquiry, with black women squarely positioned at the center. Other works like Daina Ramey Berry's *"Swing the Sickle for the Harvest Is Ripe": Gender and Slavery in Antebellum Georgia* and Mary Farmer-Kaiser's *Freedwomen and the Freedmen's*

Bureau: Race, Gender, and Public Policy in the Age of Emancipation continue to elucidate black women's historical struggles against both sexism and racism. They further illuminate their civil, political, and educational activism in ways that demonstrate that despite their historical marginalization, they speak soundly to black women's agency, autonomy, and resistance, as they were more often than not leaders, rather than followers, in critical community uplift efforts. This scholarship expertly probes the contours and nuances of the world from black women's perspectives and again asks that critical question, "Can the sistas get some history, too?"[4]

This activist framing is echoed in important scholarship that has had a profound effect on my thinking about black women's activist labors in myriad Southern communities and institutions. Harvard University scholar Evelyn Brooks Higginbotham's 1994 monograph, *Righteous Discontent: The Women's Movement in the Black Baptist Church, 1880–1920*, for instance, was the first account of black women's critical roles in cultivating churches as activist spaces. As African American–owned and operated institutions, black churches were the primary sites for social and political efficacy and community self-help and uplift. Because, as Higginbotham notes, black women constituted the majority of African American church congregations, they astutely crafted "public sentiment" and "expression of a black collective will" in ways that allowed them to wield considerable social, economic, and political power in their communities. I have a photograph of me and Dr. Evelyn Brooks Higginbotham in February 2018 after I gave a presentation on rural black women at The HistoryMakers board meeting in New York City. Headquartered in Chicago, The HistoryMakers is the largest African American digital oral history archive.[5]

While not exclusively focused on the South, Bettye Collier-Thomas's groundbreaking and exhaustively researched book *Jesus, Jobs and Justice: African American Women and Religion* (2010), builds on Higginbotham's work by chronicling a diverse array of black women as activists in churches and through such organizations as the African Methodist Episcopal Zion Church's Women's Home and Foreign Missionary Society, and also across racial lines and through such female-centered and -led organizations and the Young Women's Christian Association and Church Women United. Collier-Thomas also examines black church women's experiences as the founders of the National Association of Colored Women and the National Council of Negro Women. She chronicles marginalized leaders in male-dominated organizations such as the NAACP, of which at least two black women, Mississippi's Ida B. Wells-Barnett and Memphis, Tennessee's Mary Church Terrell, remained largely unheralded as its cofounders.[6]

And speaking of Ida B. Wells-Barnett and Mary Church Terrell, studies abound about the former but less so about the latter. Paula J. Giddings, Mia Bay, Patricia A. Schechter, and Sarah Silkey, among others, have published works that have fleshed out the contours of Wells-Barnett's life and activism. That is less the case with Terrell, with the exception of Joan Quigley's *Just Another Southern Town: Mary Church Terrell and the Struggle for Racial Justice in the Nation's Capital* (2016) and my own chapter, "Mary Church Terrell: Revisiting the Politics of Race, Class, and Gender," in Sarah Wilkerson-Freeman's and Beverly Bond's edited collection, *Tennessee Women: Their Lives and Times* (2009).[7]

Scholars have recognized both Wells-Barnett and Terrell as national leaders, and I would advocate that educator and activist Mary McLeod Bethune also is an exemplar of this leadership within and beyond Southern black communities. As a black female leader, she skillfully and at times, according to Bethune biographer Joyce A. Hanson, contradictorily reached across the racial morass of Southern apartheid to obtain critical support for her initiatives. Whatever her methods, Bethune employed this strategy to found the Daytona Educational and Industrial School for Negro Girls in Florida in 1904 and the National Council of Negro Women in 1935. Both were specifically established to develop black women as leaders who were then expected to become uplift advocates in African American communities nationwide.[8]

This body of work, among others, has profoundly sharpened our understandings of the intellectual labor in which black women engaged as they carefully assessed and navigated the temporal and geographical times in which they travailed. In doing so, they empowered themselves and their communities through their individual and collective, community, and institutional activism. They challenge scholars of Southern black women's history to explore the silences that often reveal so much about the complexities of their lives in deeply and often hostile racialized contexts.

Much of the aforementioned scholarship centers on black women with Southern roots who either left the South entirely or moved back and forth between the South and urban areas. I am keenly interested in black women who lived most of their lives in Southern locales where they recognized both the problems emanating from racial apartheid and African American subordination and the viability and vitality of these spaces where the histories of local subaltern resistance and activism had long been evident. My personal critique is that some of this recent scholarship has focused almost exclusively on black women's lives and labors in Mississippi. This body of work includes the publication of Chana Kai Lee's *For Freedom's Sake: The Life of Fannie Lou Hamer*, Francoise Hamlin's *Crossroads at Clarksdale: The Black Freedom Struggle in the*

Mississippi Delta after World War II, Crystal Sanders's *A Chance for Change: Head Start and Mississippi's Black Freedom Struggle,* and Tiyi Morris's *Womanpower Unlimited and the Black Freedom Struggle in Mississippi.*[9] Now please do not misunderstand me: these are important works that either center or prominently feature black women in their analyses, but black women's experiences in Mississippi do not speak for the entire South. The South is not ubiquitous, and neither are Southern black women's stories.

The literature of the civil rights movement has included some of the struggles of black women, but only recently have scholars of the twentieth century begun to highlight neglected aspects of the field. Pioneering works such as Belinda Robnett's *How Long? How Long? African American Women and the Struggle for Civil Rights* (1999) and Barbara Ransby's *Ella Baker and the Black Freedom Movement: A Radical Democratic Vision* (2003) have been followed by a diverse and powerful outpouring of rich new interpretations of women's contributions to this critical era.[10] Danielle McGuire's prizewinning *At the Dark End of the Street: Black Women, Rape, and Resistance—A New History of the Civil Rights Movement from Rosa Parks to the Rise of Black Power* (2011) opened up new debates about the role of sexual violence in African American women's daily lives during the twentieth century.[11]

Even so, the extant scholarship on the twentieth-century South has so far not pushed the analytical envelope on rural black women's experiences. But, the sands are shifting.

Melissa Walker's *All We Knew Was to Farm: Rural Women in the Upcountry South, 1919–1941,* and Lu Ann Jones's *Mama Learned Us to Work: Farm Women in the New South,* both of which include discussions on rural black women, provide a critical intellectual grounding for my own interest and inquiries in this area.[12] How do we understand rural Southern black women inside and outside of oppressive contexts as conscious actors and determiners of their own fate? How do we give volume to those voices and stories that have been muted within the Southern historical landscape? As I read Melissa's and Lu Ann's books, I thought deeply about how to heighten an awareness of rural black women's lives when there are few available records.

So, I am going to discuss my own scholarship, because I think female historians are often reticent about promoting themselves in this hetero-patriarchal profession. Is that all right? My first book, *Crossing the Line: Women's Interracial Activism in South Carolina during and after World War II,* was reflective of these questions and significantly transformed, again, how I research and tell Southern black women's history.[13] By looking at women such as Sara Z. Daniels, a South Carolina Agricultural Extension Service home demonstration agent who lost her job because of her civil rights activism, I learned that agricultural records were ripe with stories about rural black women's lives as health, educational, and political activists.

In my recent turn to Arkansas history, I discovered interesting and diverse women about whom woefully little had been written, which resulted in my co-edited volume, *Arkansas Women: Their Lives and Times.* My primary interest, however, and the subjects of my next book (*Better Living by Their Own Bootstraps: Black Women's Activism in Rural Arkansas*) are the many black women who were rural activists as home demonstration agents, Jeanes Industrial Supervising Teachers, and members of the Arkansas Association of Colored Women.

Southern black women's connections to national events is important, as well. Living and working in Arkansas has afforded me access to a plethora of untapped resources and opportunities to chronicle these unexpected forays onto the national stage. Take, for instance, Thelma Burke, a funeral home owner in Forrest City, Arkansas (located in the Delta and named after Confederate general Nathan Bedford Forrest), who in 1951 was placed on the House Un-American Activities Committee's watch list because she, along with W.E.B. Du Bois, Pablo Picasso, Marc Chagall, and others signed the 1950 Stockholm Appeal calling for a ban on nuclear weapons. I have further had the distinct honor of meeting and befriending at least one of the women I write about, Mrs. Annie R. Zachary Pike, a farmer and significant landowner in rural Marvell, Arkansas, who is alive and quite well at eighty-seven years young, thank you very much. In the 1960s, she served on the United States Department of Agriculture's Citizens Advisory Committee on Civil Rights and in 1972 ran for the Arkansas state senate as a Republican. This was after her stint as the Phillips County Republican Party coordinator, which helped elect New Yorker Winthrop Rockefeller as Arkansas's first Republican governor since Reconstruction.

Again, Arkansas women's experience must not be viewed as the total or even the emblematic experience of black Southern women, but these contributions texture and embellish appreciation of the ever-expanding richness of recent scholarly interrogations. We must think *strategically* about how we access the resources to tell Southern black women's histories, because much of it traditionally has not been available in privileged and mainstream, "read white," archives and repositories. Let me again use Annie Zachary Pike as an example. When I began my research on her life and activism, the only thing I found about her in the archives was her name on a list in the Republican Party of Arkansas files and a flyer from her 1972 campaign.

When I discovered she was still alive, I of course *immediately* called her.

The first few times she hung up on me. *Why wouldn't she?* She didn't know me from Adam's house cat, and she had absolutely no reason to trust me. And, in case you are not aware of this, older black women are often very suspicious of those who contact them wanting to "tell their stories for them." I knew I could not just show up at her house because, number one, it's rude and, number two, Ms. Annie, as everyone calls her, remembers well how dangerous the rural South was and still is for African Americans. What I rightly assumed and later found to be very true was that Annie Zachary Pike's home was highly weaponized because rural black people have always believed in armed self-defense as a means of survival. An intermediary eventually connected us after I had been vetted and found to be a member, like Ms. Annie, of the Order of the Eastern Star, Prince Hall Affiliated, and the Arkansas Association of Colored Women. You see, community connections matter.

I interviewed Ms. Annie, after she fed me a ginormous meal that gave me the "itis." (Look that up in the urban dictionary if you don't know what it means.) I scanned documents that are available only in her home and was essentially adopted as a member of her family. The last time I went down to Marvell, Arkansas, they sent me back to Jonesboro with a big old bag of purple hull peas.

Now that's enough about my ongoing scholarship. 'Cause I'm not about to show you all of my cards and tell you all of my tricks, and, as the singer Erykah Badu once said, "Now keep in mind that I'm an artist (Or, in my case a historian!) and I'm sensitive about my shit."[14]

But what is patently demonstrable is that the Southern history field is in dire need of scholarship about black women who lived their entire lives in the twentieth-century rural South and about their intentionality in navigating it across a racist, classist, and gendered spectrum to implement impactful change in ways that still, to this day, have gone largely unrecognized. Southern black women's history is rampant with scholarly opportunities. And I would like to provide some additional thoughts about the directions in which this area of study could and indeed should go.

I have read and thought long and hard about the scholarship produced by Brittney Cooper, in particular her 2017 publication *Beyond Respectability: The Intellectual Thought of Race Women*, and how we/I can better mesh intellectual and Southern black women's history.[15] Cooper considers the intellectual development of such fairly well-known Southern-born black women as Mary Church Terrell, Anna Julia Cooper, and Pauli Murray, among others, with much alacrity and acuity. But what might such an analysis look like if we considered intellectual history from the perspective of Southern, black, female agriculturalists, for instance, for whom it was impractical to employ respectability politics, let along reach beyond them? How, indeed, did Southern black women, particularly those who resisted the migratory tide to urban locales, make sense of a world where racism, sexism, and particularly the threat of violence were omnipresent?

How did women, who by and large lacked formal education, craft a language to articulate their frustrations, hopes, and dreams? How do we distill their language in ways that help us understand that "dialect does not equal intellect" and that, in the case of agrarian women, "rurality does *not* equal ignorance"? A shout-out to my colleague Dr. Jenny Barker Devine for that one.[16] How can we, as scholars, better excavate, read, and thoughtfully interpret their long-standing invisibility in the historical record? These inquiries, for me at least, will be partially informed by Keisha N. Blain, Christopher Cameron, and Ashley D. Farmers's edited collection *New Perspectives on the Black Intellectual Tradition*.[17]

The other questions I pose are as follows: Who besides Blain Roberts, in *Pageants, Parlors, and Pretty Women: Race and Beauty in the Twentieth Century South*, has written about Southern black beauty pageants as racial agrarian activism?[18] I know, for example, that in Arkansas, Daisy Bates, whom we all know about from the 1957 Little Rock Central High School crisis, was a sponsor and chaperone for the Spirit of Cotton contest, a phenomenon from 1948 to 1956 as the analogue of the white-only Maid of Cotton Contest. The former simultaneously celebrated black women's beauty and African Americans' roles in cotton production.

And what about Southern black female internationalists? Studies by Gregg Andrews, Dayo Gore, Carole Boyce Davies, and Keisha Blain in *Set the World On Fire: Black Nationalists Women and the Global Struggle for Freedom* (2018), which focuses on Louisiana-born and Arkansas-raised Mittie Maude Lena Gordon, have elucidated black women's internationalism in their struggle against white supremacy.[19]

We must continue to mine nontraditional resources for Southern black women's voices so that we may highlight, as Blain suggests, "the creative and critical ways women articulated black internationalism during the twentieth century."[20] We should be intentional about ascertaining how these women connected global analyses of oppression to their own lived experiences.

To conclude, we must boldly, aggressively, and creatively question how we research Southern black women's lives. We must consider their positioning in contexts where we tend not to expect to find them. We must assume that they were present and involved, because they almost always *were*, and think expansively about where sources on their lives and activities are housed. We must explicate the ways that we can and should understand and consume the diverse perspectives embedded in Southern women's history.

Some of you might not believe that fat meat is greasy, but believe me when I tell you: this scholarship is long overdue and there is much work to be done to fill the gaps in the historiography and provide Southern black women's history with increased visibility. Let's allot them their proper place in the historical narrative by generating studies that center their experiences so that the "sistas can continue to get some history." In this way, we might unceasingly transform Southern women's history generally by continuing to productively complicate the breadth and depth of the field.

Notes

1. PRELIMINARY REMARKS: Good afternoon, let me start by saying how very happy and honored I am to be with you today. I would especially like to thank Catherine Clinton for asking me to be a part of this symposium. I am humbled to be included among scholars whom I deeply respect and whose work has significantly informed my own. Thank you, Bill Link, for making all of this possible and a special high-five and thank you to David Meltsner for taking care of all of the logistics. Now let's get down to business, shall we?

2. I am a proud member of Sigma Gamma Rho Sorority Incorporated.

3. See Deborah Gray White, *Ar'n't I a Woman: Female Slaves in the Plantation South* (New York: W. W. Norton, 1999); Tera Hunter, *To 'Joy My Freedom: Southern Black Women's Lives and Labors after the Civil War* (Cambridge, Mass.: Harvard University Press, 1997); Stephanie Shaw, *What a Woman Ought to Be and to Do: Black Professional Women Workers during the Jim Crow Era* (Chicago: University of Chicago Press, 1996); Paula Giddings, *When and Where I Enter: The Impact of Black Women on Race and Sex in America* (New York: W. Morrow, 2007); Darlene Clark Hine, *Hine Sight: Black Women and the Re-Construction of American History* (Bloomington: Indiana University Press, 1991); Daina Ramey Berry, *Swing the Sickle for the Harvest Is Ripe: Gender and Slavery in Antebellum Georgia* (Urbana: University of Illinois Press, 2010); Mary Farmer-Kaiser, *Freedwomen and the Freedmen's Bureau, Race, Gender, and Public Policy in the Age of Emancipation* (New York: Fordham University Press, 2010); Thavolia Glymph, *Out of the House of Bondage: The Transformation of the Plantation Household* (New York: Cambridge University Press, 2008); and *The Woman's Fight: The Civil War's Battles for Home, Freedom, and Nation* (Chapel Hill: University of North Carolina Press, 2020).

4. See also Cynthia M. Kennedy, *Braided Relations, Entwined Lives: The Women of Charleston's Urban Slave Society* (Bloomington: Indiana University Press, 2005); Wilma King, *The Essence of Liberty: Free Black Women during the Slave Era* (Columbia: University of Missouri Press, 2006); Emily West, *Family or Freedom: People of Color in the Antebellum South* (Lexington: University Press of Kentucky, 2012); Sharony Green, *Remember Me to Miss Louisa: Hidden Black-White Intimacies in Antebellum America* (DeKalb: Northern Illinois University Press, 2015); Virginia Meacham Gould, *Chained to the Rock of Adversity: To Be Free Black and Female in the Old South* (Athens: University of Georgia Press, 1998); Jessica Millward, *Finding*

Charity's Folk: Enslaved and Free Black Women in Maryland (Athens: University of Georgia Press, 2015); Amrita Chakrabarti Myers, *Forging Freedom: Black Women and the Pursuit of Liberty in Antebellum Charleston* (Chapel Hill: University of North Carolina Press, 2011); Judith Kelleher Schafer, *Becoming Free, Remaining Free: Manumission and Enslavement in New Orleans, 1846–1862* (Baton Rouge: Louisiana State University Press, 2003).

5. Evelyn Brooks Higginbotham, *Righteous Discontent: The Women's Movement in the Black Baptist Church, 1880–1920* (Cambridge, Mass.: Harvard University Press, 1994)

6. Bettye Collier-Thomas, *Jesus, Jobs, and Justice: African American Women and Religion* (New York: Alfred A. Knopf, 2010);

7. Paula J. Giddings, *Ida: A Sword among Lions: Ida B. Wells and the Campaign against Lynching* (New York: Amistad, 2009); Mia Bay, *To Tell the Truth Freely: The Life of Ida B. Wells* (New York: Hill and Wang, 2010); Patricia A. Schechter, *Ida B. Wells-Barnett and American Reform, 1880–1930* (Chapel Hill: University of North Carolina Press, 2001); Sarah Silkey, *Black Woman Reformer: Ida B. Wells, Lynching, and Transatlantic Activism* (Athens: University of Georgia Press, 2018); Joan Quigley, *Just Another Southern Town: Mary Church Terrell and the Struggle for Racial Justice in the Nation's Capital* (New York: Oxford University Press, 2016); Cherisse Jones-Branch, "Mary Church Terrell: Revisiting the Politics of Race, Class, and Gender," in *Tennessee Women: Their Lives and Times*, vol. 1, ed. Sarah Wilkerson Freeman and Beverly Bond (Athens: University of Georgia Press, 2009), 68–92.

8. Joyce A. Hanson, *Mary McLeod Bethune and Black Women's Political Activism* (Columbia: University of Missouri, 2003).

9. Chana Kai Lee, *For Freedom's Sake: The Life of Fannie Lou Hamer* (Urbana: University of Illinois Press, 2000); Francoise Hamlin, *Crossroads at Clarksdale: The Black Freedom Struggle in the Mississippi Delta after World War II* (Chapel Hill: University of North Carolina Press, 2014); Crystal Sanders, *A Chance for Change: Head Start and Mississippi's Black Freedom Struggle* (Chapel Hill: University of North Carolina Press, 2016); Tiyi Morris, *Womanpower Unlimited and the Black Freedom Struggle in Mississippi* (Athens: University of Georgia Press, 2015).

10. Belinda Robnett, *How Long? How Long? African American Women and the Struggle for Civil Rights* (New York: Oxford University Press, 1999); Barbara Ransby, *Ella Baker and the Black Freedom Movement: A Radical Democratic Vision* (Chapel Hill: University of North Carolina, 2003); Bettye Collier-Thomas and V. P. Franklin, *Sisters in the Struggle: African American Women in the Civil Rights-Black Power Movement* (New York: New York University Press, 2001); Bruce A. Glasrud and Merline Pitre, *Southern Black Women in the Modern Civil Rights Movement* (College Station: Texas A & M Press, 2013).

11. Danielle McGuire, *At the Dark End of the Street: Black Women, Rape, and Resistance—A New History of the Civil Rights Movement from Rosa Parks to the Rise of Black Power* (New York: Knopf, 2011). For an earlier era, see Crystal Feimster's *Southern Horrors: Women and the Politics of Rape and Lynching* (Cambridge, Mass.: Harvard University Press, 2009).

12. Melissa Walker, *All We Knew Was to Farm: Rural Women in the Upcountry South, 1919–1941* (Baltimore: Johns Hopkins University Press, 2002); Lu Ann Jones, *Mama Learned Us to Work: Farm Women in the New South* (Chapel Hill: University of North Carolina Press, 2002).

13. Cherisse Jones-Branch, *Crossing the Line: Women's Interracial Activism in South Carolina during and after World War II* (Gainesville: University Press of Florida, 2014).

14. https://www.azquotes.com/quote/849673.

15. Brittney C.Cooper, *Beyond Respectability: The Intellectual Thought of Race Women* (Urbana: University of Illinois Press, 2017).

16. Jenny Barker Devine is associate professor of history at Illinois College and the author of *On Behalf of the Family Farm: Iowa Women's Activism since 1945* (Iowa City: University of Iowa Press, 2013).

17. Keisha N. Blain, Christopher Cameron, and Ashley D. Farmer, eds., *New Perspectives on the Black Intellectual Tradition* (Evanston: Northwestern University Press, 2018).

18. Blain Roberts, *Pageants, Parlors, and Pretty Women: Race and Beauty in the Twentieth Century South* (Chapel Hill: University of North Carolina Press, 2016). See also Maxine Craig's *Ain't I a Beauty Queen?: Black Women, Beauty, and the Politics of Race* (New York: Oxford University Press, 2002); and Tiffany Gill, *Beauty Shop Politics: African American Women's Activism in the Beauty Industry* (Urbana: University of Illinois Press, 2010).

19. Gregg Andrews, *Thyra J. Edwards: Black Activist in the Global Freedom Struggle* (Columbia: University of Missouri Press, 2011); Dayo Gore, *Radicalism at the Crossroads: African American Women Activists in the Cold War* (New York: New York University Press, 2012); Carole Boyce Davies, *Left of Karl Marx: The Political Life of Black Communist Claudia Jones* (Durham, N.C.: Duke University Press, 2008); Keisha N. Blain, *Set the World On Fire: Black Nationalist Women and the Global Struggle for Freedom* (Philadelphia: University of Pennsylvania Press, 2018).

20. Keisha N. Blain, "Readings on Black Women's Internationalism," in *Black Perspectives*, aaihs.org (accessed November 22, 2019).

/

5

Present at the Birth of a New History

A Southern Midwives'Tale

GLENDA ELIZABETH GILMORE

To say that I've grown old over the past thirty-odd years with the Southern Association for Women Historians (SAWH) might be an overstatement, but only because I was older already when I became a historian and joined in 1988.[1] As a nervous thirty-nine-year-old graduate student, coming from a career in business, I had never encountered an organization remotely similar to the SAWH. By joining at that historical moment, I caught a wave of revolution that changed our profession and transformed our understanding of the past. It was the birth of a new kind of Southern history, of a new way of looking at the past that radically and permanently reinterpreted our understanding of it. The SAWH generated, drove, and sustained this wave.

In the 1970s and 1980s, historians of the U.S. South witnessed the consolidation of the new field of Southern women's history. Of course, some historians had written about women in the South before that time, most often as biographical treatments of particular women and sometimes to note women's contributions to aspects of the Southern experience. However, from 1970 to 2000 and beyond, a pioneering generation of historians of Southern women reconceived of women's roles in the South, began to reinterpret the South's history through a gendered analysis, wrote influential articles and monographs, and trained robust generations of graduate students. The SAWH was founded in 1970, on the cusp of an exponential increase in the national percentage of women who earned the history Ph.D.—from 11 percent in 1969 to 43 percent in 2014. These women historians promoted women's history, and a gendered view of Southern history produced a vibrant field. They opened new positions in the academy and assured a place for women in the archives, in the classroom, and in public discourse.[2]

The awakening owes a fundamental debt to the Southern Association for Women Historians. It brought together previously isolated women historians in the South and historians who worked on Southern women to validate first their existence and then their field. Megan Shockley, SAWH president in 2017, put it this way, "We are an organization born out of an activist mission to assist women historians and advance women's history. We are here to support our members. We mentor each other."[3] *We mentor each other*. I find that an extraordinary truth in a profession built on competition for the chance to earn a livelihood, on historiographical arguments that all too often involve gate-keeping, and on an elitist hierarchy that eschews *collaboration* in writing and teaching history.

The association is a case study that is almost unique among historical associations. It was *not* founded on the basis of the profession as a whole, as was the American Historical Association (AHA). Nor was it founded on a geographical field alone, as was the Organization of American Historians or the Southern Historical Association (SHA). Women who write and teach in the South in fields other than Southern history are a vital part of it. Nor was membership exclusively limited to women. In some ways, it was the original ally organization. In 1985, the SAWH changed its name from the Southern Association *of* Women Historians to the Southern Association *for* Women Historians to make it clear that male historians eager to support women's history and female historians who did not write about the South were and had always been welcome. In fact, Thomas Appleton and Jonathan Daniel Wells both coedited conference volumes, a heroic and often thankless task. Nor was the SAWH founded on the basis of a specialty, such as the Oral History Association or the Society for Historians of American Foreign Relations. Finally, the SAWH was not meant to be an organization exclusively for university professors: from the beginning, many public historians and independent scholars, for example, Sandra Treadway of the Library of Virginia, a tireless member and president in 2002, and Elizabeth Jacoway, an independent scholar, were vital contributors.

So why then was the SAWH founded? The following photograph makes the reasons for its founding abundantly clear.

This is the executive council of the Southern Historical Association in 1980. The lone woman in the photo is Carol Bleser, a founding SAWH member and its president in 1998. It's tempting to read this photograph as an historical document. The man on Carol's right might be mildly unhappy that he has to kneel.

The man on Carol's left is seated with what we can only hope is a *paternal* hand on her thigh. And I don't even want to speculate on the placement of the gavel above her head. But Carol Bleser certainly looks eager.

The SAWH's 1970 founding document articulated its goals this way: "to study and advance the status of women at all levels of the historical profession; to oppose discrimination against women in the profession; to encourage the teaching of women's history, and to develop research in the field; and to disseminate information on research grants, fellowships, and other aids to professional advancement for women."[4] The SAWH goals echo those of the Coordinating Council for Women in the Historical Profession (CCWHP), which had grown out of the American Historical Association a year earlier, in 1969.

It is important to note that the SAWH was not a separate organization at its founding. The model that it first embraced was as a "women's caucus" for the Southern Historical Association, as the CCWHP did for the AHA. That activist group challenged business as usual in the AHA, which CCWHP leader Bernice Carroll described as "a gentlemen's protection society . . . openly supporting practices of sexism, racism, classism, heterosexism, and antisemitism." Carroll saw the CCWHP as "an independent Women's Caucus, quite apart from any official AHA Committee or resolutions adopted by the AHA, to thrash out all that needs to be done."[5]

Likewise, the SAWH operated as a caucus within the SHA until 1975, when it decided that it could develop the field of Southern women's history and its own institutional stability better as an associated organization of the SHA, raising its own funding and doing its own work, some of which involved helping the SHA evolve. That crucial 1975 decision meant that the SAWH had to take a key role in developing female leaders and required it to think at every turn about what a feminist organization should be and do.

Moreover, while the CCWHP split into two organizations in 1974—the original CCWHP would become the professional advocacy group and the Conference Group on Women's History promoted research and writing in women's history—the SAWH kept both functions under the same structure. This synergy proved extremely productive. Some SAWH members who joined simply because of their interest in Southern women's history quickly realized that to love their topic, they had to advocate for it and for themselves in the profession. The model of activist scholars who fought on two fronts—to write history and to champion their standing in the profession—gave graduate students like me an object lesson in walking the walk, not simply talking the talk. Activism and scholarship became two sides of the same coin, something that—believe it or not—I had been afraid to do in my new profession. It also fostered an anti-elitist structure within the SAWH. We lambs could lie down with the lions—the women who wrote the texts we were reading in class—on a committee and watch them speak openly about discrimination within the profession and how we could fix it. And the lions could depend on many lambs to do a great deal of organizational work. Our very scarcity in the profession meant that we needed all of the female power we could get. This was a new kind of professional organization, one devoted not to gatekeeping but to throwing open the gates. And the SAWH, much more than the SHA, embraced public activists—women who made history themselves. I met Anne Braden, civil rights activist, Virginia Durr, New Dealer and author, and Texas governor Anne Richards at SAWH events.[6]

Of course, a large part of the SAWH's agenda for thirty years was to open up the Southern Historical Association to women's full participation and to achieve recognition for women's history. As historical associations go, the SHA was small, warm, and, at least superficially, courteous. It was almost familial, and therein lay the rub. A member called another member when a job became available at his institution and asked his friend to send his best grad student over to fill it (this was AHA and OAH practice as well). The SHA itself had struggled with its own professional status, trying to wrest Southern history out of the hands of hagiographers, sentimentalists, and generations of Lost Cause cultists since its founding in 1934. As late as 1935, when C. Vann Woodward was in graduate school at the University of North Carolina, Vann studied with *the only man born outside the South* who was teaching American History in the entire region: Northern-born Harold K. Beale.[7]

By 1970, the SHA had its own contingent of radical male historians who had participated in the civil rights movement, who had begun to tell the truth about race in Southern history, and who sought to include the voices of non-elite actors. People like Woodward, Joel Williamson, and John Hope Franklin had been writing truer Southern history for at least two decades by the time that the SAWH was founded. That did not necessarily mean that everyone in the radical camp was ready for women's history. As historian Gerda Lerner said about the AHA and the CCWHP, "radical history was a chosen viewpoint, based on philosophical, social, and political commitments. . . . It was different for women historians in the early years. . . . We represented half of the population, . . . [yet we] were not even considered legitimate outsiders—we had yet to prove that the work in our field had any significance."[8]

On that note, I recall explaining my work in *Gender and Jim Crow* on an elevator at the SHA around 1991, literally giving an elevator talk, when my interlocutor, himself a radical Southern historian, responded, "Oh, okay. But didn't Steve Stowe write *the* book on gender and Southern history?" Indeed, Steven M. Stowe had written a marvelous book, *Intimacy and Power in the Old South*, but it was about intimate lives, manhood, and the *Old* South.[9] I had just explained that my work was on black women, the *New* South, and how gender worked in politics that institutionalized Jim Crow. In my companion's mind, there was room for one book on gender in Southern history, and it had been written. As late as the early 1990s, Southern historians had no conception of the tsunami of Southern women's history that was to come pouring down on them.

The SHA had always officially been open to women and African Americans. W.E.B. Du Bois was a member. Nonetheless, although three women had been among the twenty founders of the SHA in 1934 and "formed 25% of its membership in the early years," executive council positions and the presidency rarely went to them.[10] There were only two female SHA presidents in the thirty-six years before the SAWH's founding: Ella Lonn in 1946 and Katherine Abbey in 1953. Mary Elizabeth Massey became president in 1972, after the SAWH's founding, succeeding John Hope Franklin, the first African American president, in 1971.[11] Lest we think that problem has been solved, roughly 22 percent of the SHA presidents—ten in forty-six years—have been women since Massey's term, during a period when the number of history Ph.D.s who were women increased from roughly 11 percent to 42 percent. The organization did not have a black female president until Darlene Clark Hine held that office in 2003. In the past twenty years, the SAWH has had three black female presidents: Jacqueline Rouse (2001), Beverly G. Bond (2012), and Barbara Krauthamer (2018).[12]

In 2018, 44 percent of the SHA executive council members are women. That percentage would indicate that five decades of work, largely done through and at the behest of members of the SAWH, has paid off. But it has not been linear

Table 1. Participation in the Southern Historical Association by Gender, 1934–1985 (Percentages are percentage female)

Year	Executive Council	Committees	Program (Overall)	Program Chairs	Paper Presenters	Program Commenters
1934–1935	20%	15%	8%	0%	0%	33%
1940	15%	8%[1]	10%	14%	5%	20%
1946	8%	4%	2%	0%	6%	0%
1950	8%	26%[2]	7%	7%	6%	—
1955	8%	6%	3%	0%	6%	0%
1960	8%	5%	3%	0%	4%	5%
1965	0%	9%	4%	0%	7%	3%
1970	0%	4%	6%	6%	10%	2%
1975	0%	17%	15%[3]	10%	18%[3]	17%
1980	7%	16%	19%	23%	17%	20%
1985	13%	19%[3]	22%	16%	24%	23%

Notes: [1] 4% unidentified.

[2] 3 % unidentified.

[3] 1 % unidentified.

Source: A Statistical Report on the Participation of Women in the Southern Historical Association, 1935-1985. *The Journal of Southern History*, Vol. 52, No. 2 (May, 1986), pp. 282–288. Published by: Southern Historical Association. Stable URL: https://www.jstor.org/stable/2209671

Table 2. Participation in the Southern Historical Association by Gender, 1980–1985 (Percentages are percentage female)

Year	Executive Council	Committees	Program (Overall)	Program Chairs	Paper Presenters	Program Commenters
1980	7%	16%	19%	23%	17%	20%
1981	7%	15%	16%	12%	15%	20%
1982	7%	17%	14%	14%	18%	12%
1983	7%	27%	22%	20%	25%	18%
1984	6%	18%	20%[1]	24%	22%[2]	19%
1985	13%	19%[1]	22%	16%	24%	23%
Average (1980–1985)	8%	18%[1]	19%[1]	18%	20%[1]	18%

Notes: [1] 1 % unidentified.

[2] 2% unidentified.

Source: A Statistical Report on the Participation of Women in the Southern Historical Association, 1935-1985. *The Journal of Southern History*, Vol. 52, No. 2 (May, 1986), pp. 282–288. Published by: Southern Historical Association. Stable URL: https://www.jstor.org/stable/2209671

progress. Despite the fact that "women formed about a quarter of the membership in the early years" of the Southern Historical Association, into the 1980s, female members were few. In 1975, SAWH members A. Elizabeth Taylor, La-Wanda Cox, and Mollie Davis presented a "Report on the Status of Women in the Profession" to the SHA. By the next year, the SAWH, which had become an affiliate organization of the SHA, began pushing that organization to include more women on committees and the executive council.[13] It seems to have made little difference in the figures shown here up until 1985.[14]

However, after that, particularly after the first SAWH conference at Converse College in 1988, the SAWH began to win recognition for its members and its goals within the SHA. It did not come naturally; the SAWH had to organize at every turn. I remember being in a very awkward meeting with Catherine Clinton and John Boles, the editor of the *Journal of Southern History* and a lovely man, in which we presented him with some hand-drawn charts on the paucity of female authors and articles on women's history in the *Journal* that embarrassed all of us. The SHA Committee on Women has now been expanded to the Committee on Women, Gender, and Sexuality. The Committee on Minorities in the Profession came in part through SAWH work in 1997.

I've just written the introduction for a forthcoming book on the pioneering generation of Southern female historians, all active in the SAWH, that is centered around breaking silences about their personal experiences and dedicated to telling radical truths about being female historians in the South. One woman recounts her first Southern Historical Association conference. She got all dressed up for her first reception, marshaled her nerve (because she knew no one there), and attempted to mingle. When she spotted the name tag of a professor she did not know personally, she introduced herself and gushed that she loved his book. He responded, in what she called "the most casual way possible" by "asking in the vernacular" if she wanted to have sexual intercourse.[15] In 1998, Catherine Clinton's long campaign for an SHA policy on sexual harassment finally came to fruition. The SAWH transformed the SHA. But it took at least three decades.

The way that happened is a lesson in organizing and organization building: the SAWH built a lean, mean feminist machine in the 1980s, one that its members continue to stoke today. There is much to be studied in its model, but five features stand out: the office of the organization's secretary; the triennial conference; intense graduate student involvement; formal recognition of work in Southern history and women's history; and the annual SAWH address and party at the SHA.

In 1985, Darlene Clark Hine advocated for an institutional home and a working secretary who, through an agreement with her home university, could be freed from some teaching and/or committee work and given an office supported financially by her department. Newsletters, conference support, and membership management had become huge tasks, not to mention coordinating the campaigns for new initiatives. Institutionalizing the organization in one place with one person for terms of several years was the only way to insure continuity among elected officers and smooth running of the organization. The organization would not have survived without this office and structure.

Melissa Walker also hosted the first triennial conference at Converse College in 1988, and it has become the embodiment of the SAWH's goal to combine activism and scholarship in ways that nurture women. Of course, it was modeled on the Berkshire Conference, but, from the start, it was quite different. Most of the participants were members of the SAWH—we knew each other—so there was plenty of room and time to talk about activist aspects of the organization while presenting scholarship. Everyone was interested in almost every paper— there weren't really subfields—so navigating concurrent sessions proved to be agony. We stayed on college campuses, so when you snuck away to the pool at 6:30 a.m. with a cup of coffee and a cigarette, you ran into Anne Scott swimming laps. It remains a conference that particularly welcomes graduate students, and there could be no better audience for workshopping a paper. I've made many of my best friends over the years at these conferences; it's history camp—a rock 'n' roll cruise—for female scholars. There's no swanning around here: communal showers, lost soap, hard beds, and frank talk. Anne Scott once told me there to cut my hair to look more professional, and Sally McMillen told me that my earrings were too large to get a job. They were both (probably) right.

When four hundred people showed up at the first conference in 1988, I was a graduate student; it was my first spend-the-night conference and my first conference paper.[16] I was terrified. I was presenting a paper on black women's suffrage in North Carolina, and my copanelist, Wanda Hendricks, discussed Chicago black women's politics under the leadership of Ida B. Wells-Barnett's Alpha Suffrage Club. When we came into the room, Darlene Clark Hine and Anne Scott were already sitting beside each other in the front row and Darlene was wearing sunglasses. It was all the more meaningful because, just three years earlier, Wanda and I had worked together in business in Charlotte before either of us decided to pursue a Ph.D.

Now, we figured if we could make it here, we could make it anywhere. My talk that day became part of *Gender and Jim Crow: Women and the Politics of White Supremacy in North Carolina, 1896–1920*, and Hendricks's work was key to her book, *Gender, Race, and Politics in the Midwest: Black Club Women in Illinois.*[17] The 1988 program included a good deal of the new, field-changing, work in black Southern women's history, and that has remained the case at subsequent conferences.[18] On a panel that A. Elizabeth Taylor chaired, Marjorie Julian Spruill's paper, "Southern Suffragists and the 'Negro Problem,'" became a major argument in *New Women of the New South: The Leaders of the Woman Suffrage Movement in the Southern States*.[19] Adele Logan Alexander's presentation on Adella Hunt marked the beginning of her exploration of her grandmother's life, and her monumental biography of Adella Logan Hunt was published by Yale University Press in the fall of 2019.[20]

The tradition of including marginalized scholarship continues. The 2018 conference underscored how much offerings on Native American women, Latina women, and sexuality have grown over the years. So have sessions on digital history, including public scholarship through an online presence, and public history, which was the conference theme of 2015 in Charleston. Interestingly, sessions on food are up-and-coming.

The third key to the SAWH's success is that it does not simply welcome graduate students; it invests in them. If graduate students are an organization's lifeblood, the SAWH is Dracula. If they choose to be active, they enroll in a boot camp in leadership. I'm not the only person who started as a grad student on the graduate committee—at the behest of Marjorie Spruill, who worked me to a nub—and became president of the organization. For years, the graduate committee passed down the SAWH beer cooler, which a committee member took to Sam's Club to fill up with drinks and celery sticks for the grad student party at the conference. Through these "best practices," the SAWH kept the dues low: five dollars for grad students. In 2008, it went up to a whopping ten dollars.[21]

The fourth pillar of success is the SAWH's recognition of women's contributions and work on Southern women's history through awarding four prizes and a fellowship. Each award meant that the organization had to raise a small endowment to fund it; in other words, members had to send checks and (remember, this was the old days) pressure their publishers to contribute to endow them. With each prize came more membership involvement on prize committees, building loyalty and the career-enhancing honors that these prizes bring to our members.

The SAWH's four prizes honor more than a century-long history of female historians and Southern women's history. Julia Cherry Spruill was born in 1899 in Rocky Mount, North Carolina. She graduated from the North Carolina College for Women—now UNC-Greensboro—where Bill and Susannah Link began their careers. Following her academic husband to UNC-Chapel Hill, she taught school and published *Women's Life and Work in Southern Colonies* in 1938. She lived until 1986.[22]

Antoinette Elizabeth Taylor was born in Columbus, Georgia, in 1917. At some moment, she legally changed her first name to A. because Antoinette was too long and fussy. A. Elizabeth Taylor earned her master's in Southern history at the University of North Carolina in 1940. She was accepted at Vanderbilt—she always thought it was because the men were at war—where she earned her Ph.D. She joined the faculty at Texas Women's College in 1943 and taught there for thirty-eight years. She wrote articles about the fight for women's suffrage in many Southern states; for years, her work stood alone. Her strategy—an article on the suffrage campaign in individual states, instead of a book on Southern women's suffrage—reveals a canny appraisal of her best chance to make a difference in Southern women's history. Teaching what was probably a 4/4 load at a woman's college, probably without a regular sabbatical, Taylor could use two or three summers to research and write about one state, and then move on to the next.[23]

Taylor was at the founding meeting of twenty women of the Women's Caucus in Louisville, held in the basement, "next to the boiler room." When the Women's Caucus became the SAWH in 1975, she wrote to another founder, Rosemary Carroll, "I want to congratulate you on this splendid job that you did with the women's association. I think you've put it on a sound base and it is now on its way towards becoming a lasting influence among Southern Women Historians. The new name is quite an improvement of Women's Caucus."[24] Until she died, in 1993, I saw her at every meeting of the SAWH at the SHA. Impeccably dressed, she had the most beautiful head of white curls—just like Elizabeth Cady Stanton.

Vann Woodward directed Willie Lee Rose's 1962 Johns Hopkins dissertation, and he admired her as no other historian; he often talked to me about her. She was one of the first women to crack that glass ceiling. She published the remarkable *Rehearsal for Reconstruction* two years after completing the dissertation, taught at UVA, and returned with tenure to Johns Hopkins in 1973. She was the first woman to hold Oxford's visiting Harmsworth professorship—a mere fifty-five years after it was established. She rushed home to the States that summer to give a keynote at the Big Berks. Carol Bleser was there:

I think it was 1978, we were at the Big Berks. . . . She was going to be giving a major speech, and we were going to have dinner together. Then someone came in and said, "Have you heard that Willie Lee had a stroke?" . . . All I wanted to do was to go home. I mean I still get emotional because I think she got chewed up being the only woman at that level in the field . . . she was asked to do so much. She carried the burden because there was no one else. And it's not our fault that there wasn't anybody else, but the system had only allowed for a few . . . She represented to me what happened to women, to all of us as we took on all these burdens and tried to do everything right.[25]

Willie Lee Rose was incapacitated for the next forty years until she died on June 20, 2018, at the age of ninety-one.

The Jacquelyn Dowd Hall prize, given for the two best papers presented by graduate students at the triennial conference, is a fitting tribute to Hall in two distinct ways: she writes pathbreaking conference papers that become articles, and she has devoted herself to training graduate students. I'm pretty sure that she read every sentence in my dissertation drafts five times; by the end, she was editing her own previous edits. Her care for her students was legendary. Born in Oklahoma, Hall earned her Ph.D. in 1974, at Columbia with Kenneth Jackson. She spent her career at the University of North Carolina at Chapel Hill and founded the Southern Oral History Program, which is an invaluable repository of interviews with women, civil rights crusaders, and labor leaders. Her first book, *Revolt against Chivalry: Southern Women and the Campaign against Lynching*, gave us one of the first signs that Southern women's history would not simply add accounts of Southern women to the history of the South; rather, it would demand a complete retelling of Southern history itself.

Taking the white Southern women's campaign against lynching seriously, particularly by focusing on how they sought to refute the myth that it was the rape of white women by black men that justified lynching, demanded a new explanation of Southern race relations. Her article "The Mind That Burns in Each Body" called the rape/lynch myth "folk pornography" and shook the Old Guard in the Southern to the core. Her most recent field-changing article, "The Long Civil Rights Movement and the Political Uses of the Past," is one of the most cited articles ever to appear in *The Journal of American History*. *Like a Family: The Making of a Southern Cotton Mill World*, coedited by Hall and five others, exemplified her commitment to collaborative scholarship and laid bare women's work in cotton mills. Her most recent book, *Sisters and Rebels: A Struggle for the Soul of America*, published in 2019, has already been called a "masterpiece."[26] There is much more that I could say about Jacquelyn, but I'll say only two things to bring this portrait full circle: she lives in a house that she bought from Julia Cherry Spruill's sister, and I wouldn't be standing here— I wouldn't be a historian—without her, nor would scores of other historians whom she taught and mentored.

When I was president of the SAWH, I read a startling statistic that I have long since misplaced: something like only one out of three female historians publish a second book.

I was struggling with three children, a husband/academic, and the professional model that you have to move your entire family to take most fellowships because they are residential. It seemed that a mid-career fellowship, however small, could meet an obvious need, if only to pay for three weeks at the Red Roof Inn and childcare costs while you did out-of-town research. The members agreed, and we began fundraising.

Anne Scott, born in Athens, Georgia, in 1921 was one of those women, like Willie Lee Rose, who cracked the glass ceiling. She was Phi Beta Kappa at the University of Georgia, worked on Capitol Hill during World War II, and then earned her Ph.D. at Radcliffe in 1949. *The Southern Lady: From Pedestal to Politics, 1830–1930*, became a foundational text in Southern women's history; it remains so today. She had a long career as a full professor at Duke University. Anne was the consummate professional historian—even the men were a bit afraid of her. She accepted no excuses, took her work and your work seriously, and, as we used to say, brooked no nonsense. There is nothing that she loved better than a conference, and she attended most of the SAWH conferences up to the past decade. She was a dear friend of Julia Cherry Spruill. Anne died in early 2019, at the age of ninety-seven, after the Milbauer Seminar but before this volume was published. We are forever in her debt. SAWH members are connected—in the work that they do, the advantages that they enjoy, and the struggles that they continue to face in the profession—to the generations of Southern female historians before us.[27]

Nonetheless, when you look at the women for whom the organization's prizes and fellowship are named, you see only white women. This is not representative of the SAWH for virtually all of its fifty years. It seems that the women at the organization's founding in 1970 were all white women, and by some accounts, the organization remained that way for the first few years. However, by the mid-1980s, it was far more diverse than *other* organizations and the *profession as a whole*. Part of the reason for this is the nature of Southern history. Suddenly, in the 1980s, it was impossible to write Southern history without taking into account the intersectionality of race and gender. But much of this diversity came from anti-racist protocols that the organization adopted to attract and nurture female scholars of color.

Darlene Clark Hine in 1985, Elsa Barkley Brown in 1993, Jacqueline Rouse in 2001, Beverly Bond in 2012, Barbara Krauthamer in 2018—these women have all been SAWH presidents, yet, there is no prize or fellowship to honor any of them.

Let's talk about this.

In 2017, my former graduate student, Sarah Haley, a woman of color, won both the Julia Cherry Spruill Prize and the Willie Lee Rose Prize. This year, two women of color swept the boards. Tera Hunter won the Willie Lee Rose Prize, and Sasha Turner won both the Julia Cherry Spruill Prize and the A. Elizabeth Taylor article prize, a feat never before accomplished. I recommend that the SAWH establish in the near future either a prize or, better yet, a fellowship named for one of our African American presidents—perhaps a travel fund for graduate students to the triennial conference or, more ambitiously, a larger endowment to fund a semester of stay-at-home leave for early scholars to turn a dissertation on Southern women's history into a book.

I've finally reached the fifth cornerstone on which the success of the SAWH rests. Yes, I know that there are usually only four cornerstones, but let's imagine this as the front porch, the structure through which people enter our house and stay for a while. The fifth cornerstone is the annual SAWH address and, equally important, the party that follows. The president chooses the speaker at least a year ahead of time, and it is a great honor. The annual address quickly established itself as the highlight of the entire SHA, and it's always thronged.

I'm absolutely convinced that all of the SHA members who attend, but don't belong to the SAWH, are there to soak up Southern women's history or to show their appreciation for Southern women who write history. Absolutely convinced. But it's late Friday afternoon, and they all know that the best party of the conference will follow. We made a rule that the doors of the party venue are locked until the talk is over: unless you are really shameless, you realize you should go to the talk if you want to go to the party. Several times, I've had the job of standing outside those doors and directing people who are hoping for an early drink to go over to the talk: "There's room in the back!" We also made the decision that the party is the place where we spend the money. The SHA has always hosted, shall we say, adequate receptions. But the SAWH hosts spectacular parties. This is a strategy, not an accident—just as graduate students—lambs—frequently circulate with membership forms to recruit new members at this event: with the result that lions often gift membership to their incoming graduate students to strengthen the organization's core.

Somehow in the past fifty years, while fighting discrimination, raising money, mentoring graduate students, organizing a bullet-proof organization, and honoring our foremothers, SAWH members have written great books and articles. Since their numbers are legion, I will use examples of a few books whose authors used their research in progress as the basis for giving a SAWH annual address before publication. Taken collectively, this body of work accomplished five major interventions that rewrote Southern history at large.

First, it documented the active public life of women in the South over two hundred years. For example, in 2003 Marjorie Julian Spruill gave the annual address in Houston, "Countdown to Houston: The 1977 IWY Conferences and the Polarization of American Women," that became part of her major work *Divided We Stand: The Battle Over Women's Rights and Family Values That Polarized American Politics*, published in 2017. Her cogent analysis of the divisions among women regarding the Equal Rights Amendment (ERA) and family values documents the split in the women's movement and is invaluable to our understanding of the rise of conservative women.[28]

Second, because these historians were writing at a time when feminist theoretical insights and social history methods began to link the personal and the political, their books and articles created a new genre of writing about female actors that connected the family, personal lives, civic structures, and politics. Jacquelyn Dowd Hall's 1998 address in Birmingham, "Writing a Way Home: History, Memory, and the Refashioning of Southern Identity," introduced SAWH members to the Lumpkin sisters and Hall's rendering of them as complex psychological and political figures who were shaped by the dramatic historical contexts in which they lived. In 2019, tying their personal identities to the major political issues of their time, she published *Sisters and Rebels: A Struggle for the Soul of America*.[29] The book embodies the best practices of feminist history. The personal is political, and Hall's rendering of the Lumpkin sisters' interior and public lives teaches us what it meant to be a Southern woman battered by the political tides of the twentieth century.

Third, by the 1970s, recoveries of African American history and critical insights into the intersectionality of race, class, and gender produced the revelatory insight that any topic on the American South must take into account the societal structure that bound all Southerners into mutually constitutive identities. Just as some SAWH scholars have contributed to a reinterpretation of the twentieth century, others have turned to reinterpreting Southern history through the histories of African American women. Thavolia Glymph signaled in her 1993 address a growing body of research that is rewriting Civil War history. Her talk, titled "Civil War Memoirs and the Reinvention of Black Women's History," pulled no punches with her use of the term "reinvention." Since that time, Glymph has published work from her research that transforms our understanding of the war and Reconstruction, including *Out of the House of Bondage: The Transformation of the Plantation Household* (2008). Her book *The Women's Fight: The Civil War's Battles for Home, Freedom, and Nation* appeared in 2020.[30]

Fourth, and sometimes with discomfort, writing Southern women into Southern history at large and gendering traditional interpretations presented a unique opportunity to reinterpret and revitalize the overall field. In 1999, Stephanie McCurry's SAWH address in Fort Worth, "The Brothers' War? Free Women, Slaves, and Popular Politics in the Civil War 'South,'" introduced listeners to a new, deeply gendered interpretation of the Civil War, realized in *Confederate Reckoning: Power and Politics in the Civil War South*. From her cogent analysis of "Antigone's Claim" (the problem of fighting a total war with women and children in the way) to Southern women's claims on the Confederacy, she puts women squarely in the Civil War as actors who influenced the outcome. She followed up in 2019 with *Women's War: Fighting and Surviving the American Civil War*.[31]

Fifth, this collective renaissance in Southern history transformed it from regional history into a complex body of work on how Southern concepts of race and gender operate in national politics. In 2010, Heather Ann Thompson's address in Charlotte, "Redemption Redux? Southern Politics, Economy, and Society in the Age of Mass Incarceration," connected Southern racial oppression and national mass incarceration. Her Pulitzer prizewinning book *Blood in the Water: The Attica Prison Uprising of 1971 and Its Legacy* focuses on one prison in New York, but her deep knowledge of Southern racial regimes and their national adoption informs her insights into present-day mass incarceration.[32]

It is worth pausing to remember that I selected the books I discuss here from a list of SAWH annual addresses given in the past twenty years only. Had I adopted an alternative method of discussing the effect of the Southern Association for Women Historians on the historiography of Southern history—for example, those that won SAWH prizes—I could have made the same case with different books and authors. The work is *deep* and *wide*, and it has produced a historiographical revolution.

Documenting the work of SAWH members at a rare moment—when the birth of a field that transformed first its host field and then public discourse at large—reveals important lessons about how academia transforms itself. SAWH scholars institutionalized a mentoring process in the Southern Association for Women Historians that incorporated the excitement of discovery, the hard work of self-reflection, and the process of building on one another's work. This practice happened in an extraordinarily shortened and intense time frame for a historical transformation. Both a historiographical thread and a chain of individual scholars and institutions generated a new historiography that enables our members to imagine the histories outside the traditional historical canon.

The SAWH members who collaborated over decades to transform their field built simultaneously a community of scholars who pioneered a new model of academic practice. Because this community had to be built from scratch, most often by women who faced marginalization in the historical profession, it adopted a transformative model of scholarship that is collaborative, supportive, and capacious. In a profession often rent by hierarchy, exclusion, and adversarial personal attacks, SAWH members put their collective mission first, embraced new ideas, and nurtured graduate students. They were the midwives at the birth of a history that is truer, richer, more inclusive, and vital to the problems that we face as a nation today.

Notes

1. Written in residence at Anan Cara House, Gortlicka, Dromoughty, Kenmare, County Kerry, Ireland.

2. Robert Townsend, "What Data Reveals about Women Historians," *Perspectives on History* (May 2010): 14.

3. Megan Shockley, "President's Message," *Southern Association for Women Historians Newsletter* 48, no. 1 (Winter 2017), accessed at http://thesawh.org/wp-content/uploads/2017/06/Winter-2017-Newsletter.pdf.

4. "Historical Information," Southern Association of Women Historians, 1971–2011, Collection Number 04152, Southern Historical Collection, Wilson Library, University of North Carolina, Chapel Hill.

5. Bernice Carroll, "Scholarship and Action: CCWHP and the Movements," *Journal of Women's History* 6 (Fall 1994): 70.

6. Anne Braden attended the 1991 SAWH conference in Chapel Hill, North Carolina; Virginia Durr attended a SAWH address at the SHA in the 1990s; Governor Richards attended a SAWH conference reception at Rice University in Houston, Texas, in 1994.

7. Glenda Elizabeth Gilmore, *Defying Dixie: The Radical Roots of Civil Rights, 1919–1950* (New York: W. W. Norton, 2008), 223–24.

8. Gerda Lerner, "How Women and Their Organizations Changed the Profession of History," *A History of the Coordinating Committee on Women in the Historical Profession-Conference Group on Women's History*, 43–44, accessed at http://theccwh.org/wp-content/uploads/2014/04/CCWH-History-1994.pdf.

9. Steven M. Stowe, *Intimacy and Power in the Old South: Ritual in the Lives of the Planters* (Baltimore, Md.: Johns Hopkins University Press, 1987).

10. Bethany Johnson, "The Southern Historical Association: Seventy-Five Years of History 'in the South' and 'of the South,'" *Journal of Southern History* 76, no. 3 (August 2010): 655–82.

11. Johnson, "The Southern Historical Association," 667, 669.

12. "A Statistical Report on the Participation of Women in the Southern Historical Association, 1935–1985," *Journal of Southern History* 52 (May 1986): 282–88.

13. Constance B. Schulz interview with Rosemary F. Carroll, *Clio's Southern Sisters: Interviews with Leaders of the Southern Association for Women Historians*, ed. *Constance B. Schulz and Elizabeth Hayes Turner* (Columbia: University of Missouri Press, 2004, 93.

14. Johnson, "The Southern Historical Association," 669.

15. Elizabeth Jacoway, "In Pursuit of the Dream," in *No Straight Path: Becoming Women Historians, Elizabeth Jacoway, ed.*(Baton Rouge: Louisiana State University Press, 2019).

16. Constance B. Schulz and Elizabeth Hayes Turner, eds., *Clio's Southern Sisters*, 14.

17. Glenda Elizabeth Gilmore, *Gender and Jim Crow: Women and the Politics of White Supremacy in North Carolina, 1896–1920* (Chapel Hill: University of North Carolina Press,

1996), and Wanda A. Hendricks, *Gender, Race, and Politics in the Midwest: Black Club Women in Illinois* (Bloomington: Indiana University Press, 1998).

18. *The First Southern Conference on Women's History* (Spartanburg, S.C.: Southern Association for Women Historians, 1988) accessed at http://thesawh.org/wp-content/uploads/2018/01/Program_1st-conference_1988.pdf.

19. Marjorie Spruill Wheeler, *New Women of the New South: The Leaders of the Woman Suffrage Movement in the Southern States* (New York: Oxford University Press, 1993).

20. Adele Logan Alexander, *Princess of the Hither Isles: A Black Suffragist's Story from the Jim Crow South* (New Haven: Yale University Press, 2019).

21. Laura Edwards, "President's Message," *Southern Association for Women Historians Newsletter* 39, no. 1 (Winter 2008): 1, accessed at http://thesawh.org/wp-content/uploads/2013/02/2008Winter.pdf.

22. Anna Suranyi, "Julia Cherry Spruill, Historian of Southern Colonial Women," *Generations of Women Historians*, 73–78, accessed at https://link.springer.com/chapter/10.1007/978-3-319-77568-5_4.

23. Pamela Dean interview with A. Elizabeth Taylor, in *Clio's Southern Sisters*, ed. Schulz and Turner, 21–29.

24. Constance B. Schulz interview with Rosemary F. Carroll, in *Clio's Southern Sisters*, ed. Schulz and Taylor, 90.

25. Carol Bleser interview in *Clio's Southern Sisters*, ed. Schulz and Taylor, 146.

26. Jacquelyn Dowd Hall, *Revolt against Chivalry: Jesse Daniel Ames and the Women's Campaign against Lynching* (New York: Columbia University Press, 1979); Jacquelyn Dowd Hall, "'The Mind That Burns in Each Body': Women, Rape, and Racial Violence," in *Powers of Desire: The Politics of Sexuality*, ed. Ann Snitow, Christine Stansell, and Sharon Thompson (New York: Monthly Review, 1983), 328–49; Jacquelyn Dowd Hall, "The Long Civil Rights Movement and the Political Uses of the Past," *Journal of American History* 91 (March 2005): 1233–63; Jacquelyn Dowd Hall, James Leloudis, Robert Korstad, Mary Murphy, Lu Ann Jones, and Christopher B. Daly, *Like a Family: The Making of a Southern Cotton Mill World* (Chapel Hill: University of North Carolina Press, 1987); Jacquelyn Dowd Hall, *Sisters and Rebels: A Struggle for the Soul of America* (New York: W. W. Norton, 2019).

27. Constance B. Schulz interview with Anne Firor Scott, in *Clio's Southern Sisters*, ed. Schulz and Turner, 30–50.

28. Marjorie Julian Spruill, *Divided We Stand: The Battle over Women's Rights and Family Values That Polarized American Politics* (New York: Bloomsbury USA, 2017).

29. Hall, *Sisters and Rebels*.

30. Thavolia Glymph, *Out of the House of Bondage: The Transformation of the Plantation Household* (Cambridge: Cambridge University Press, 2008), and *The Women's Fight: The Civil War's Battles for Home, Freedom, and Nation* (Chapel Hill: University of North Carolina Press, 2020).

31. Stephanie McCurry, *Confederate Reckoning: Power and Politics in the Civil War South* (Cambridge, Mass.: Harvard University Press, 2010), and *Women's War: Fighting and Surviving the American Civil War* (Cambridge, Mass.: Harvard University Press, 2019).

32. Heather Ann Thompson, *Blood in the Water: The Attica Prison Uprising of 1971 and Its Legacy* (New York: Pantheon, 2016).

Appendix A

Strange Careers: Fifty Years of Southern Women's Histories Roundtable

NOVEMBER 29, 2018
UNIVERSITY OF FLORIDA, GAINESVILLE, FL
MODERATOR: CATHERINE CLINTON
PANELISTS:
  LISA TENDRICH FRANK
  GLENDA GILMORE
  MICHELE GILLESPIE
  PIPPA HOLLOWAY
  ELIZABETH JACOWAY
  CHERISSE JONES-BRANCH
  LAUREN PEARLMAN
  CONSTANCE SCHULZ
  MELISSA WALKER

CLINTON: Well, we, of course want to begin by saying what a wonderful conference it's been. Thank you William Link, Milbauer Professor, and thank you David Meltsner for such marvelous assistance. Looking forward to our next fifty years, we think this wonderful get-together has given us so many ideas. I asked everyone to think about the first fifty years of the SAWH, to reflect on things discussed. I have asked each person to prepare a brief summary of their reflections. Then we can look strategically at how we go forward. So I hope you'll begin by stating your name and affiliation for the record. SAWH panelists—the former presidents, the former secretaries, plus other SAWH members—are gathering in Gainesville for the Milbauer Symposium, "Strange Careers: Fifty Years of Southern Women's History." We begin with Glenda Gilmore, who gave us such a wonderful talk this morning.

GILMORE: I'm Glenda Gilmore, professor emerita from Yale University. I finished [my presentation] with some admonitions about moving forward, but I didn't really get a chance to say some things about transformations in the field of Southern history. Thinking about Gerda Lerner's reflection about patriarchy dying: there was a lot of pushback. I think it was in the late 1980s, early 1990s, and people said patriarchy wasn't dying: we were fighting patriarchy all the time. Nonetheless, she was right. Patriarchy is a system whereby men as well as women are required to act in a certain way—to be patriarchal. It is designed to be an elite kind of societal structure, gendered structure, to privilege a few men, but not all men: men who are in the position to act as patriarchs. Patriarchy is dying, and I think that's really freeing for a lot of men. I want to add to what I said to comment on male allies in the SAWH. Bill Link has been an astounding ally to our work, all the way through. We have had many men within the organization who have put their shoulders to the wheel. One thing I really appreciate, the male historians who have insights that were so fundamental for our group and applied it to their own work. I think of Bryant Simons's article "The Appeal of Cole Blease in South Carolina: Race, Class, and Sex in the New South."[1] He was looking at this politics of mill hands in a new way, through insights that talk about how even seemingly inconsequential actions among men are gendered. John Howard, a great early champion when I came to the organization, was an early participant who wrote *Men Like That* about gay men in the South.[2] The work that is coming out now, like E. Patrick Johnson's *Sweet Tea: Gay Black Men of the South*, while it's not women's history, all of this came from us opening up about how gendered the Southern landscape is, and I think that's really important.[3]

At the same time, I'll just mention a couple of people: Stephanie McCurry, whose *Masters of Small Worlds* takes the idea of gender and applies it to Southern history as a whole.[4] Keri Leigh Merritt, whose *Masterless Men* thinks about how gender in Southern history stood up in Appalachia.[5] Bradley Proctor is working on gender and gender and Reconstruction, and his book should be out soon.[6] Crystal Feimster is working on sexual violence and the Civil War.[7] None of this work could have been done thirty years ago without the kinds of ideas that we sparked and the kinds of intersectionality that the work on Southern women and Southern women's work nurtured. So I'm proud of that, so proud of the men who decided that patriarchy wasn't good for them either.

CLINTON: Thank you Glenda, thanks. I think we are going to move on to Melissa . . .

WALKER: Melissa Walker, professor emerita of Converse College. I don't have a whole lot to add to all of these things we've talked about, but I would say for all of the wonderful work that has been done over the last fifty years, for all of the new stories that have been uncovered, as you said, Catherine, there are lots more sources out there and lots more methods for mining those sources than we have even thought of yet! So I think that the challenge for the next generation of historians is finding more of those stories, those little-known stories, and finding new ways to mine those archives. I just finished editing a collection of short documentary selections for the last of the books in a series that Carol Bleser founded at the University of South Carolina Press, Women's Diaries and Letters of the South. And Beth English found a set of correspondence or a set of letters written by a Virginia mill worker woman in the 1910s, the 1920s.[8] There is a lot of that kind of stuff still in the archives. In many cases, it takes a lot of work to decode it: for example, with Laurel Ulrich's *A Midwife's Tale*.[9] There is much rich material, and it is up to us to figure out how to use it. I also think that there are still big gaps in understanding the role of Hispanics and Asian immigrants in the South, particularly in the twentieth century. That's a whole rich field of potential inquiry that we need to be getting at. Lots of opportunities are out there for continuing to uncover the story of the South and the story of Southern women.

CLINTON: Thank you. Now, Betsy?

JACOWAY: My name is Elizabeth Jacoway, and I am an independent scholar who has lived and worked for many years in the tiny hamlet of Newport, Arkansas. I am grateful to Catherine Clinton and Bill Link for including me in this splendid conference and for giving me the opportunity to reflect on where the Southern Association for Women Historians has been and where it might go.

I was one of the early presidents of the fledgling organization. When I came onboard in 1978 the early battles were behind us, and the really fun activities were just getting underway. We created the first two prizes, honoring Willie Lee Rose and Julia Cherry Spruill. We started having speakers at our annual meeting and a festive reception afterward (which quickly became the best party at the Southern Historical Association meeting). We reached out to women in the profession and increased our membership dramatically. We developed a newsletter. We worked hard, and we had a lot of fun. As Melissa Walker said yesterday, we provided a venue for women to support each other and to feel valued.

Over the forty or so years since then, SAWH has made enormous contributions to our profession, and in important ways, it has changed our profession. Where the old model of a "men's club" was exclusive and competitive, we have participated in promoting the values of being inclusive and supportive. Our predecessors had to break down the barriers, but we have been able to employ a more ladylike approach, and in many ways our persistent subversion of the old values has been successful.

Now that the gates have largely been flung open, I would like to suggest that it would be helpful to our members if we would promote regional efforts to improve our writing and research. Cherisse Jones-Branch and I are involved in one such group of twenty women, the Delta Women Writers, who range along the Mississippi Delta from Memphis to New Orleans. Composed of members in their late twenties to their early eighties, we get together twice a year in Jackson, Mississippi, to read and critique four papers that have been circulated in advance. We generally have only one or two members from the same department. The tone is always friendly and supportive, but the approach is unfailingly rigorous. We have been enormously successful in seeing our work published, and that is at least in part a result of the increased confidence our work together has fostered.

I can see similar groups growing up across the South: just a quick look at the concentrations of colleges in the region suggests a D.C.–area collective, a North Carolina Triangle writing group, a Florida writers' symposium, a Kentucky-Tennessee group, an Alabama-Georgia group, a Texas collective. SAWH could help with this by suggesting the idea and facilitating the dissemination of organizing strategies and tips from other groups. The benefits would accrue to all of us, as we would be inspired to keep our eyes on the prize of productivity, and we would learn tremendous amounts from reading and discussing the work of our cohort. We have succeeded at encouraging and mentoring our graduate students. Now we could branch out into improving our own skills and productivity.

I have enjoyed my years of involvement with the Southern Association for Women Historians. I have formed wonderful friendships with women all over the region, and I look forward to seeing them every year at our annual convention, where I invariably find new friends. I am excited to think that there is more good work for us to do, and I do believe that the vitality of an organization depends on continuing to develop and pursue programs that will be of benefit to the members. I thank you for the opportunity to share my thoughts with you, and I wish you all the best.

CLINTON: Okay, thank you. Lisa. Want to state your name?

FRANK: I'm Lisa Tendrich Frank. I'm an independent scholar and I have a Ph.D. from Florida and am a former Milbauer fellow. I'm excited to be here. Thank you for including me, so do you want me to talk about how I feel about the SAWH, or where do I think it should go?

CLINTON: Both.

FRANK: Ok, the SAWH is a very comfortable place for me to be. It's wonderful to be in an environment where you can tell your stories to other women and men, who have some sort of similar experience, or at least understanding or sympathy with you. As a grad student I was advised to always go to the SHA. I find [the SHA] also to be a comfortable place. I remember going when it was all men and you would only see a couple women in there. I sort of stuck close to the men I knew, because I knew I would be protected. I did feel a bit awkward . . . and young and threatened. As a Civil War historian, I still have experiences of men just not taking me seriously. Historians assuming that women don't know anything about battles or soldiers; after all, she is just a girl, right? I keep waiting for that to go away. But when I go to SAWH conferences, it's not there. You can have any kind of conversation you want. You can! Michele mentioned the roundtables that we have done there, and they've been fabulous. The audience gets really engaged and we have these wonderful conversations that you don't always get in other environments—not at the AHA. Maybe you have a couple of people willing to listen, to expand the scholarship of the Civil War into things that include gender and women. My focus is on the interaction between soldiers and women. It's not just women's history specifically but trying to look at everyone's relationship to gender. A lot of Civil War scholars say that doesn't matter, you know: just look at the troop movements, or what the soldiers thought they were doing because those details are all that matter. So SAWH is a place that gives me the sort of confidence to be able to do what I want to do.

When we talk about sources, you have to go to sources that aren't listed in any of those guides for women's history or gender history. I just go through as many things as I can. At this point, I know what I am looking for . . . nobody catalogs that, so it's not often listed in any of the finding aids. But I can find what a soldier is saying about a woman and find fifty soldiers saying similar things. I can find women writing in their diaries, and then, you know that this was important to everyone . . . It didn't just get glossed over. I would like to see the SAWH have more inclusivity on panels—I think on Native Americans, Latinas, and such. I'm married to a historian of Native America and at each conference, he's "oh look, there's two Native American panels; they are always at the same time." Or "they have got their one Native American panel." I think there are a lot of fields like that. Because most people aren't doing those fields, they are not as noticed. I think the program committees must get better at finding more people from different fields. Now, it is easier for me to get on a program because people recognize what I do, but there are a lot of fields out there where people are still struggling.

CLINTON: So if you don't mind me asking, two of you have been navigating this notion of an independent scholar. There is a lot of debate over whether you use that language, or not. I'm not going to really get into that, but I want for you to comment on the SAWH in terms of being someone who is not formally at an institution or within a department? I'm really asking about the role of independent scholars within our organization. Do you have any comment on that?

JACOWAY: I just said to Melissa a few minutes ago, the SAWH has been my network and has been my way to stay connected. I learned a long time ago that if you go to the conferences and you wore your name badge, and you visit with everybody, no one knows if you go back and teach classes. The important thing is to *publish*, to be there, and to *participate*, and *contribute*, and to *publish*. And it really doesn't matter if you don't have a teaching job.

FRANK: Although I would say that the SAWH is more accepting of independent scholars, I get asked a lot, [my husband is at FSU (Florida State University)] . . ."You're not at FSU too?" or "why aren't you teaching?" At SAWH, people are more okay with that, more than if you go to AHA. People are not going to talk to you if it doesn't say a university on your name tag, unless they already know you, at least in my experience. But, I also think that once you publish, it becomes much easier.

JACOWAY: Right.

FRANK: I had published essays, but before my book came out, people didn't really know if they were going to give me the time of day. They usually didn't! But not at SAWH, because there are so many different levels of people from public history, for example. There is not that judgment factor that you get from some of the larger conferences.

CLINTON: Okay. Thank you. Cherisse?

JONES-BRANCH: I agree with everything that's been said . . .

CLINTON: Your name, please.

JONES-BRANCH: Cherisse Jones-Branch, professor of history, Arkansas State University. And, I agree with everything that's been said. While you were talking, Lisa, I was really thinking about name recognition and what it means in other organizations. And, I distinctly remember going to conferences with an Arkansas State University badge, and people taking one look at me and deciding I wasn't worth talking to! That's not an experience I've had at the SAWH. From the very beginning, I've found it to be an incredibly supportive organization. I often think about the group of women I'm in with Betsy Jacoway, the Delta Women Writers group: I believe we are all members of the SAWH. And so, between that organization and the SAWH, I've been blessed to work with colleagues who have been incredibly supportive. They give really important feedback about your work—not intended to shred anyone's self-esteem but to really help you grow as a scholar. I think that's important, along with the fact that I've grown and matured and come to understand that's what most of these folks want to do: they want to help you do your very best work. It's also because of that that I have met people like Melissa Walker. I have read her work, and, as I said yesterday, reading that kind of work made me realize that, yes, there are other areas that I can go into when talking about women, particularly black women's history. It has allowed me to do things I never imagined possible. So I went from being a member of these groups to discovering there's a rural women's studies association—and the agricultural history society! So there were other places where people would understand and respect my work: that wasn't necessarily happening in other organizations.

I mean, I focus on rural black women. I go to black history conferences: no one has a clue about what I'm talking about, nor are they particularly interested. But I have not found that to be the case with these two organizations and these women. We need to make sure that we are a more inclusive organization. I think part of my issue early on as a member of the organization [SAWH] was that I was very intimidated.

I was young and naive, and over time I have worked through a lot; because of the people I have met in this organization, I take it on as a personal responsibility to guide people through who might feel the same way I once felt some twenty-odd years ago. That's a hard thing to get over, particularly when you don't feel like you have anybody who's going to help you. You don't imagine you have the right to ask for the help that you need. And so in my mind, this has been a great organization, for all of those reasons. One of the things I'm going to do as soon as I get home: I know a couple of young female scholars who are working on their doctorates and for Christmas they are getting memberships to this organization. They're like: "We don't have the money." Well, that's okay. I do. And I'm going to make this happen for you until you can get to a place where you can do it, and it is your job to pay it forward. But those are the kinds of lessons I've just learned as a member of this organization.

CLINTON: You mentioned writing, so I would like to come back to it after we hear from everyone. You mentioned writing, and Glenda described how important that was to mentor for SAWH conferences: sent a paper ahead of time, we had the personal responsibility, which you signed up for, to work with someone. This goes on at our triennial conferences, but perhaps it is something so valuable and considering the timeline for graduate students, it might be something we can incorporate into the annual SAWH agenda. Perhaps there is a way, every year, you know, in addition to "the cooler and the bucket" [a reference to SAWH providing grad student refreshments] you know, a way of easing people into the profession. Next, Michele.

GILLESPIE: Michele Gillespie, Wake Forest University. I have such great faith in this organization in that I think the next ten, twenty-five years are going to be amazing. I have no worries at all about the exciting ground the scholarship is going to cover and the new ways we are going to continue to push and press women's and gender and sexuality history. . . . I really appreciate what my colleagues have said about finding new voices and really being more inclusive and having that represented in our conferences and the work that we do. And I really agree with Glenda in talking about the radical nature of this organization and how it creates a very different model for professionalism, in history and in academics in general. Even as I say these things, I want to remind people that higher ed. is not going to look anything like what higher ed. looks like now. Twenty-five years from now we are going to see some enormous changes in how academics work, and I don't know what it is going to look like for history. I don't know what it's going to look like for Southern history and Southern women's history. I'm concerned about what's going to happen with states' budgets. I'm concerned about the rising cost of tuition. I'm concerned about the kind of consolidations of schools and the kinds of consolidations of academic departments we are going to see. And, I'm concerned about the number of faculty that are going to be contingent [adjunct faculty, non–tenure track appointments]. So I would ask the SAWH to think, since we are radical, since we are activists, to really be thinking about what that means. How are we going to take care of contingent faculty? As supportive as we are of independent scholars and of public historians, what are we going to do for the contingent faculty? What are we going to say to institutions as this happens more and more? And how do we support them when they're doing four-four teaching loads? So, to that end, I have a couple of other pragmatic ideas I want to share with you all. One of the things I noticed is a lot of other organizations give out teaching awards. We've always focused on scholarship, and I think that is wonderful and important. But when we look at the work that we do, can we think about offering an award in teaching that shows the innovative, imaginative, effective ways colleagues are incorporating gender, sexuality, women studies, not only in women's history or gender, but in all of their courses. So could we kind of showcase how you can do that through a teaching award? We can also honor those faculty who are at those places who cannot necessarily get their scholarship done at the same rates as other folks. . . . We know because of the work we do as Southern historians that local is global. So can we be thinking about ways in which the SAWH can help make more connections between the scholarship we do and our teaching and what is happening at the local levels? So how can we promote the value of what we bring to the table with the communities that we work in and communities around us: ways we can support in terms of helping understand neighborhoods and community building. We can be listening to our neighbors in our communities tell us whose voices *aren't* at the table and how to make that happen. What tools do scholars need, and how can we help them find them? I think a lot about the work that so many of you have done around this table today based on oral history. I know you have given, after you have finished your projects, you have given your oral histories to different schools. Could we have an SAWH oral history project? Where have SAWH members put their oral histories? Perhaps at UNC with the Southern Oral History Program? Under the rubric of the SAWH? Could we think a little more inclusively? We're doing so well in professional development, but I think we can do even more on alternate careers and have that sort of front and center in the things that we are doing. And then, the last thing I'm going to say, and Glenda, I thought you nailed it: Resources, right? I mean, being able to have the financial resources to have the independence to do what we have done is really important. And I think if this organization is really smart, we are going to get savvier. I think we can probably be thinking much more about doing our own development work, our own advancement work. I think we should be looking at talking to our colleagues about their estates and what relationship they might want to have with the SAWH. Giving their estates to us—or pieces of their estates—to support the radical, important, significant work that we are doing. So I would really challenge us to think about how we can incorporate that, *integrate* that into the work of this organization. That will give us even more latitude to do more of this good work.

CLINTON: Great. Thank you. But I'm going to ask you a little more. Why don't you tell about your project with Reynolda and your students, to give our audience an idea about how you sent them out into the community?

GILLESPIE: Oh, okay . . . sure, sure.

CLINTON: I know people are interested in this idea, so give us a practical example. We'll give you a little more time.

GILLESPIE: Connecting outreach to teaching: my example of connecting my teaching and scholarship. I was working on a book project on Katharine and R. J. Reynolds during the early twentieth century in Winston, North Carolina, and their contributions to the cultural, political economy. I focused on their decision-making, and their leadership, and the challenges.

I was able to invite my students to do a lot of work with me—including a lot of demographic work. We did neighborhood work: we went to assisted living communities and did oral histories. And so I was really able to showcase: we were reading big-picture pieces and the students were doing the research with me and connecting it with what we were reading. And I was able to share with them my chapters as I was developing them, showing them how the work that they were doing contributed to my work as well. And the very act of aligning my teaching and my scholarship meant that I wasn't finding teaching exhausting [laughter in background]. . . . Everything fit together beautifully, and I have a lot more energy for all of it. I think my students found excitement in my passion for what I was doing and they found ownership in their work in the source: they were writing their own papers out of it even as I was using the material. So I think there are really exciting ways, with the right kind of resources, to integrate your teaching and your scholarship that benefits everybody. And I also like to think that the book benefited the community as well.

CLINTON: Great. Now to you, Pippa! My head is overflowing with all the great ideas.

HOLLOWAY: All of our heads are overflowing, I think. Since I didn't have the pressure to give a talk this weekend, I've had the great opportunity to take a lot of notes and I want to take this as a brief opportunity to connect—literally—some of the notes that I took and questions that I had written in the margins over the last couple of days. It started with Michele's talk: when one of the provocative things that she said—talking about how histories of women, gender, and sexualities have reshaped the Civil War—is "how they *haven't*." How the public discourse of the war, to some extent, hasn't incorporated the amazing scholarship done in women's history. And what I wrote in the margin was that we live in a historical moment that's authorizing a particular set of power relations about whiteness and gender, right? This is the white male moment, in a sense, trying to resurge. And also a moment in which there is an overt rejection of facts and truths [laughter in background] but that particular set of people that are trying to run our country again. And it makes me think about this larger question we have been asking, about how the history we write is connected to and part of the present. We always write history for the present—just as they too are trying (to the extent I can consolidate the Trumpets of the world into a "them,") to write histories for the present—that they're also trying to produce. That got me thinking, then, when Glenda spoke. I thought one of the many, many provocative things she put up was that chart about how there's a decline in women's participation in the SHA during the Cold War: I think you called it "the Cold War chills." That was really striking because, you know, to think about how the present is shaping literally the kinds of histories we write, the kinds of historians writing them. Which then got me thinking about what we are doing, in light of what many of y'all spoke about: what we have done throughout this period as women's historians is to aggressively and intentionally write the kind of histories that we think that matter. We are trying to create stories to shape the present—for example, Catherine's discussion what we are collecting and archiving, that, too, is a part of this. People who are doing the collecting and archiving are, again, part of this larger project. Melissa, there is a line in your talk that really resonated with me and made me think about how not only what is being written is important but also what is being *read* is important. Reading each other's work is also part of that! Who we authorize, whom we assign, whose work are we talking about at a conference. Have you read this great book by x, y, or z . . . that is also part of what we do, the kind of promotion of each other's work. That is what really struck me in Cherisse's talk because what you did was really bold. You put people's work up there and you said these are the books that are being written, that matter to our scholarship. And it struck me as you were doing it that this was a kind of political act, a very savvy one in fact. All of that got me thinking back to the idea of what the SAWH is about, what the scholarship is about. We aren't and mustn't be victims of the historical moment, but we should be agents of it! A lot of the work that people here have been doing is pretty intentional about that. Two related notes as I close: one is one of my pet peeves, the idea of using "evolution" as a term to describe what happens in history because it suggests a passiveness alongside progressiveness, right—that things keep getting better. "Cold War chills." The other one, just to get it off my chest: I don't like the "bending-toward-justice" thing, because history doesn't "bend toward justice." You've got to sort of put your shoulder into it and shove it! *We* bend it toward justice. Which, then, got me back to the last thing, which is, a better environmental metaphor, one that worked a little better for me was Glenda's comment in which she described a "tsunami" of Southern women's history. [laughter in background] I think I would like to move from "evolution" to "tsunami" as the environmental metaphor I would choose as appropriate for the kind of scholarship that we do and will continue to do.

CLINTON: I like "tsunami," but I also more approve of "wave" [laughter in background] . . . as Nancy Hewitt. . . .

HOLLOWAY: Take it down sometimes.

CLINTON: But Nancy Hewitt, discussing second-wave feminism, used language about "waves" and "radar." Spreading words and finding the metaphor for second-wave feminism, third-wave, and so on. Because "tsunami"—to some people—hints at disaster and I don't think we want to talk about the "disaster" of our work cascading, or descending, but I think you may be right, as many of my Civil War colleagues are for "rubble" and, ah, reminding people of what was there before and what will come after, so maybe that is a good metaphor . . . But, Connie? You want to share with us?

SCHULZ: I'm Connie Schulz, professor emerita at the University of South Carolina, but I am also the senior editor and project director of the born-digital scholarly editions of the papers of Eliza Pinckney and her daughter Harriet Pinckney Horry. After we did the women, I am now editing the papers of Pinckney statesmen.[10] And I give those as my credentials because that's related to what I want to say. Michele said we don't know what the academic environment is going to be in twenty-five years. We *really* don't know what the publishing environment is going to be. How are your books going to be published? Where are your articles going to appear? And I would like to make a push that the SAWH becomes involved in helping to usher in and legitimize the use of these digital technologies for publishing in the future—just as it legitimized the field of Southern women's history and the field of Southern black women's history. We need to be showcasing it, reviewing it, and highlighting it. My editions have never been reviewed in the *Journal of Southern History*. Even though we invite them to review: there has never been a positive response. My colleague Holly Shulman, who is editing the papers of Dolley Madison, a digital edition, a born-digital edition, has been trying for fifteen years to put together a collaborative—calls it "federal editing." There are hundreds of examples of papers of women, which increasingly gains significance as the public cannot read cursive handwriting—that needs to have editions for the students in university classrooms to be able to read those papers. Holly's idea was that we could do a sort of collaborative edition of the papers of founding women—people of the founding era who were women who wrote, who exchanged letters—where are *their* papers? If small, individual editors did the papers of one woman, and we put them all on the same platform, and then we created a system—just as the University of Virginia has their collection of the papers of Founding Fathers. If we had founding women together on a similar digital platform, we could look across all of their experiences—in childbirth, in nursing sick soldiers, and in participating in politics—all of the things that women did. She [Holly Shulman] has yet to get either the National Endowment for the Humanities [NEH] or the National Historical Publications and Records Commission to agree that this is a good idea. She and I have been working on this for the last fifteen years. So my plea is to think not only about topics but also about the means by which we promote and publish our scholarship. We should provide a place safe to say, "Okay, I'm going to do a series of blog posts on agricultural women . . . black women workers." Sometimes there isn't *enough*. Sometimes you build up to a book, maybe a digital book, by a series of smaller efforts. Maybe it will be tweeting [laughter in background] but maybe not. Maybe in a larger form? But the SAWH can have a role in moving into the future, in the ways that historians disseminate their work—make it available, make the voices of the past available. I'm specifically interested in editing and editions. I would also like to say about the symposium, just very briefly. My role in the SAWH has been not as a scholar presenting papers particularly, but, you know, being on the committees and doing the nitty gritty. We conducted oral history interviews, and when you're down in the weeds doing the work, you often don't see how important it is overall to a lot of people. This symposium has said to me, "Gee, we really *did* do something." It was important. And I would end with that thought.

GILMORE: If I could pick up on that, that brings to mind another possible area of SAWH activity, which is advocacy. So much of the time, as a profession, we leave the advocacy to the folks at the OAH. But something like this digital repository of women's documents is something that, *if* you and Holly were making a big push at the NEH and the NH . . .

CLINTON: PRC . . .

GILMORE: NHPRC [laughs]. You can call on the SAWH to issue some kind of statement of support and ask lots of us to sign it. And there might be other areas of advocacy. For example, advocacy on behalf of student unions or graduate student unions that our organization might consider undertaking.

SCHULZ: And I didn't say it, but I will now, the profession needs to take seriously the role of scholarly editors as making important contributions. We encourage young women or young men scholars to do scholarly editions of the writings of people whose work, whose thoughts, won't otherwise be accessible or available.

CLINTON: Great. So we *have* come up with a great number of ideas. I just want to add a few thoughts before opening up to our audience. I find it so useful to go to the SAWH and hear people talk about their teaching. Michele reminds us that women's history has been particularly good at advocating for the engagement of students in undergrad research, and I've gotten so many ideas. One of our SAWH stalwarts, Jessica Brannon-Wranosky, who's working on the Texas History Handbook—incorporating women into the project—helped me recently. When I was first teaching and I had students consult the Schlesinger Library, to search the *Notable American Women* reject file—because that was a great resource of women who didn't make it into the first volume. And I would have them do research on it as an exercise. And they would all come back and say how *hard* it was. I remember doing reference work in my graduate years and early career, and I don't remember who referred to the significance and importance of such tasks early on, but it's so important. So here I was, Tom Dublin and Kitty Sklar were doing outreach with their Alexander Street project, and combined with the Handbook of Texas Women online, I said, "Oh, great," and I handed out names of Texas female suffragists for their writing assignments, part of their graduate seminar grade. Undergraduates, as well as graduate students, can be actually creating history—and that will steer them into history. Volunteering should be done carefully, but don't dismiss working on reference books. That's where we really can make dramatic changes. I have the benefit of working in a department that is supported by a great benefactor,

John Nau, who has one of the largest private collections of Civil War artifacts and documents. In collaboration with his archivist, Sally Anne Schmidt, I have my undergraduates read selections of his collected Civil War letters. They get very excited about it and I can say with even greater excitement that Michelle Krowl, the librarian specialist at the Library of Congress, is soliciting for volunteers to transcribe Civil War letters (letters to Lincoln, Clara Barton letters, and disabled soldiers' writings).[11] Students can go online and transcribe them.

Another important shift I wrote about in my presidential address for the SHA, "The Southern Social Network," *never* turned down an opportunity to be on a prize committee. Think carefully about how you appoint these prize committees if you get a chance. I was very pleased to appoint several all-women committees for major prizes at the SHA. Glenda was talking about changes, and I would say the change in prizes over the past few years has been dramatic.

When we gave prizes and began that process in the 1980s, we felt a need to have a prize for the best book in Southern history written by a woman [The Willie Lee Rose Prize]. There were many who objected to that—women as well as men. I was reading in our archives the correspondence from Carl Degler, who felt very disappointed by this. I think it would be a great thing if we considered in the future the way in which our organization could still give the Willie Lee Rose Prize in a way that would truly honor her in the twenty-first century. She was such a leading scholar and suffered as some might have said a debility from being the "only one," but now we have a collective and we might think about a way we can give a first book prize or some other way we can shift with the times. Because looking at prizes, things have definitely changed—and I speak from having frequently been invited to be on juries, and it's such a great privilege. From my first one in the early 1980s, serving on a Pulitzer Prize jury, which was quite bruising—and I also wrote about it in my SHA presidential address: being bullied and mansplained in a committee of three. But it taught me a lot. I reached out to a network, found someone on the Pulitzer board encouraging me to offer a dissenting opinion—and in that way a book in women's history was recognized widely and did do well. The author has gone on to become a great friend. Thirty years later I served on an all-female jury for the Frederick Douglass Book Prize. That year's prize was shared by two female authors.[12] It was so interesting and important to me that the books that were emerging at the top of the list were the books I couldn't have imagined when I first started with the SAWH. Books about the enslaved, the struggles for freedom, about identities and intersectionality that are defining the field, changing the field. I was particularly heartened that many of the books nominated during this particular year—by Tera Hunter, by Daina Ramey Berry, by Sharla Fett, by

Deirdre Cooper Owens, by Leigh Fought—had already won prizes from other major organizations, committees, juries. But we'd love to hear from *you in the audience* for what you're looking for in the next fifty years in Southern women's histories. We have a younger audience than perhaps the collective age of us up here. So, if anyone out there would like to chime in? Lauren, can I ask you?

PEARLMAN: Sure . . .

CLINTON: Let's identify yourself.

PEARLMAN: Sure, I'm Lauren Pearlman, an assistant professor here at University of Florida. I was struck by Glenda's chart showing statistics about tenure and promotion for female scholars and what percentage of them finish their second book. We know mid-career scholars, female scholars, are doing a lot of service work. In fact, here in our department, service roles, from chair, associate chair, graduate coordinator, associate graduate coordinator, are filled with women, in part, because of our male colleagues saying, "Well, I'm not good at administrative work." Well, neither am I, [laughter in background] but I'll learn on the job. *But,* on the flip side, you can oversee change when you're doing these roles. You advocated and demonstrated—on the executive committees—you can make crucial changes for future scholars and address systematic problems that you see. So how do you balance doing this work that makes a change with advancing your career in other ways that are more publicly recognized in terms of scholarship.

CLINTON: I used to say "just be incompetent, like the men, and it will work for you." That didn't really work. Satire often doesn't. But trying to, you know, work within what you are given, and you are only given a certain amount of power within each committee. As a woman junior faculty member, you must do everything you can to improve your position, even if it only gives you a marginal amount of power, but serving on committees can be good. Recently a couple came into my department and the woman was asked to serve on *seven* committees and the man was assigned only three committees. They have the same rank. You know, so the woman comes to me and I do think senior women need to play a role in such situations. And it came out of a conversation: "How are things going?" You do have to ask people because people don't often want to come to you first thing with complaints. So seeking out senior women in the department, if there are senior women, is a great strategy. Or seeking out those advocates that Glenda talked about—finding men in power positions who are advocates for bringing women into departments and advancing them. Maybe others have . . .

GILMORE: You know we have a thing in our tool kit that I worked on [online SAWH toolkit]—about how to say no and how your department may not know that the university has asked you to serve on a committee, etc. So that's worth looking at and saying "no" to those fifth, sixth, and seventh committees. But also, and this is a harder thing, because you can't tell what's coming—but life has seasons and there are seasons when you want to be senior essay director. That was the toughest job I ever did at Yale. You know, being president would have been easier than senior essay director. There are seasons—issues in the graduate program that need fixing so you're DGS [Director of Graduate Studies]. There are seasons when you can go out and be more active in the profession—and life is very long, so my rule was not to repeat those service things, which is not to say that I'm so egotistical that I thought, "Well, if I went in and fixed it and you can't keep it fixed, that's your problem." But actually, I did. There is no use for repeating things that didn't work *the first time*—so try to make a difference, try to build in the structure that will make your difference stick. If it looks like an intractable problem, just move on. Go do something else where you can be useful, rather than repeating failures of not being able to reform X, Y, and Z about your department or university.

WALKER: With a lot of my coaching clients, I work on this issue and we talk a lot about what Glenda said, about seasons. And there are also seasons in your personal life where you may have young children, you may have to care for elderly relatives, and you have to take that into consideration as well. But I think it's also a matter of your own priorities, and for some people that internal service is more satisfying than, maybe, producing another scholarly book—or at least at this stage in their career. As Glenda says, so you have to evaluate your own priorities. But the other thing is that you have to speak up, as Catherine said, and you have to find someone senior and say, "I need some help because I've been asked to do this and this and this, but I'm already doing these three other things, and I can't do them all well. And so, I need some help figuring out what should be the priority for the department, and for the institution." You throw the onus back on somebody else to help you navigate that service burden. Because I think, Glenda's right, a lot of times departments don't know what you are doing in the university that is a source of stress and tension and overwork.

GILLESPIE: And there may be a way to get at this that not only helps you but also helps the institution as a whole. At my school, we have created a survey instrument for every faculty member where you list what department committees you're on, what college committees you're on, what university committees you're on, and so we can document it by department and we can give this to chairs, and say, "Oh my, why is it that seventy-five percent of the women associate professors are doing seventy-five percent of the work?" So it documents and takes it away from you, the individual, to show these larger patterns. It can help to create institutional change for everybody.

CLINTON: There is a great strain there because you do read documents for promotion to tenure and for promotion to full professor, which always include service as a component, including "community service." I get quite angry at this fiction, because I have sat on committees where I've seen it disregarded. Unless you are on a very high-ranking national committee, you must instead focus on the university and have boxes ticked. Research and publicity is at the top of the pyramid, and yes you could have stellar teaching, but more significantly, and this is the problem, these components may be given equal weight in black and white—but in reality research is the one thing by which particularly historians are really judged. So if you don't talk to people and you don't consult, you are often getting bad advice because it's a department chair's business to fill those committees—and to diversify committees, to be the untenured person on search committees is often a strategy that is just frightening for people. Do keep in mind that consulting with, you know, a strong senior person in the department who has navigated what you navigated is often one of the best ways to survive.

JONES-BRANCH: And I think it's important, as a senior scholar—there was a moment when I woke up and realized I was a senior scholar. And I remember when I was fresh out of graduate school! But I think it's important for senior scholars to reach out to younger scholars as well. One of the things that I noticed at Arkansas State [University] in the past few years is that a number of young African American scholars just left the university. By the time I found out what was going on, they had already resigned and were on their way out. So now I make it a practice . . . you know, I don't nag. I don't want to be intrusive; I'm not trying to get in your business. But, you know, just an email saying, "Hey, you ran across my mind. How are you doing? Let's have lunch," or something like that. And I really do mean for it to just be lunch—and then, two and a half hours later: you are going through this, you're going through that, and how do I navigate this and that? And sometimes it's just enough to just listen and to let them work through what's going on. But there have been moments where I have had to say, "Well, you can't respond to this in a certain way at this point in your career but I can. So let me talk to this person. We go way back . . ."—whatever. Sometimes things can be resolved in that way, as well. But I think, I think the onus is on me personally to be mindful of newer and younger colleagues and what they might be going through. And I think you make a choice about that, because when I first went to Arkansas State I didn't have that, but I made damn sure the folks coming after me had it.

CLINTON: I want to go back to something we talked about yesterday and was touched upon by Connie today—that is the publishing field in Southern women's history. We talked quite glowingly about our series at Missouri, which is a wonderful series but, again, has now been shuttered. We talked about this incredible series at Georgia that Nancy Grayson spearheaded and shaped, then taken over by the wonderful Lisa Bayer—now suspended. We are in a real publishing crisis: we as an organization cannot command our own series, I believe, even at a university press. As university presses are being defunded, made accountable to a bottom line; they are in crisis. So can we give some insight for people hoping to publish in Southern women's history and what we see besides the documentary platforms that Connie was proposing. Does anyone have any other strategies or ideas that they would like to share? I know, Lisa, you've recently done a reference book, and so maybe you can . . .

FRANK: I would not recommend doing a reference book . . .

CLINTON: Yes, you're not going to recommend a reference? No.

FRANK: Well, I think they are valuable, but they suck up a lot of time.

CLINTON: Right.

FRANK: I was doing that because I wasn't teaching—so I had the time to do it . . .

CLINTON: Were you building up a corps of people, though? I mean, does it . . .

FRANK: I had some people, but when working on encyclopedias, you have a hundred and fifty, two hundred, authors to herd like cats. It's all great at the beginning but the ends of those projects . . . [laughter in the background] . . . are really kind of a nightmare. I've told many people here that by the end of all three of these encyclopedias, my husband and I became experts on all sorts of things: women from colonial times to the present, including female veterans of the Iraq War. . . . I think contributing to them is a good way to build up a CV for younger scholars. Much to my chagrin, they don't pay much, unless you write a whole lot. I fought with the press, but these are always for-profit presses doing them—and they don't really pay me, and they don't give me any money to pay contributors. So you have to decide how much it's worth to have that line on your CV. If anyone wants to edit an encyclopedia, contact me, I'll tell you the highs and the lows.

CLINTON: So, sales, you know, *is* a real burden for publications, and it is showing up at university presses. What about participation on academic journals, on editorial boards. I've edited many collections, and I thought people knew me as an editor. But, for example, I've never been invited to be on the board of the *Journal of Southern History*. I'm asking my colleagues who have been on these boards—boards at journals, boards at university presses. Like Wake Forest has a press . . . [laughter in background]

GILLESPIE: It's an Irish literature press . . . [laughter in background]

CLINTON: There you go. . . . [laughter in background]

GILLESPIE: It's very, very narrow [laughter in background]

CLINTON: Go ahead . . .

HOLLOWAY: I was on the board of the, not of the Southern, but of the *Public Historian* for two different terms. And being on those boards allows you to encourage certain kinds of participation. It's like being on a program committee—you are able to spot things that come in, not only to see things that people are volunteering, but you can encourage people to fill in gaps: topics or ideas that aren't there. Being on a board as an editor, as things move toward the digital, increasingly journals are going to be born digital—not just digitized by JSTOR. We need to be, as an organization and as a field, active in two ways—to advocate in two ways. One is to encourage the creation of digital platforms as the more traditional ones disappear. Young scholars won't have a place to publish their work or to make their work available to the public. Second, to make that kind of scholarly performance legitimized within whatever areas, in museum reviews or in promotion and tenure cases. Those, too, are going to change. But we have to legitimize those alternative ways of getting your scholarship out there.

CLINTON: Right, right . . .

HOLLOWAY: I'll just drop in real quick that all of us do a ton of article and manuscript reviews and that's one of the most thankless jobs of the profession . . . [approving crosstalk by panel]. You're anonymous and no one knows you do it. You slave away at the articles, with "I'm trying to help you make this better" . . . [laughter in background]. Then they get mad at you, then it's like "these comments are terrible." . . . I don't have a lot of graduate students, and for me it's been an opportunity—surreptitiously and clandestinely—to encourage and shape the work of younger scholars . . . what gets published and what is part of the canon of our profession. So to get back to your comment, it's an important service task that's often not even acknowledged.

GILMORE: I want to add one thing. I'm a series editor for the University of Pennsylvania Press, and many of you have been series editors. For Penguin Press, and at UPenn Press, we have a great interim step. The series editor actually edits the manuscript, so I was asked to read Keisha Blain's book *Set the World on Fire*, before it went out to readers, which I did. I did a full manuscript treatment, and I think that really helps an author understand where an author's work fits into a field because they have gotten such a deep read. They haven't just gotten a three-page thing. So, if more presses could do that, it would be great. If you want to get involved in being a series editor, being actually a hands-on editor, that's great. The only other thing we have to realize is how Blain promoted that book. [panelist agreeing in the background] She got it out there. We've never had a book in the series that has sold as much, and it absolutely deserves it. Everybody deserves to see that! She reached out digitally and by speaking at every venue she could find: made her book a bestseller for a historian. And I haven't done that with my past two books. I just haven't. You know, you just get to the point . . . [laughter] . . . and presses have very little publicity built in anymore. I heard from my publicity agent for *Defying Dixie* once . . .

CLINTON: I think we all have learned to depend on our own resources—I know the University of Georgia Press has been pleased with the sales of *Medical Bondage* by Deirdre Cooper Owens, and if you follow her on Facebook as I do, you know, where in the world is Deirdre? Fewer and fewer presses are able to go to conferences. The SAWH began in the 1980s to have book sales—not only was it a way to raise funds, but many people had books coming out and their presses could *not* come to the book exhibit. Therefore, they would be willing to send and donate some copies to the book sale. I know it went away for a while, but it's coming back again. It does take a lot of volunteering. Glenda was remembering hauling books. But I thought it was fun to push the luggage cart through the exhibit [laughter in background], and collect those books. It wasn't fun afterward when they didn't sell. Nevertheless, I think it's important.

But, I'm wondering, in talking about this, perhaps the subvention issue comes up. Is that something the SAWH could take on as a fundraiser? We have a fundraising committee and we are looking forward to the next few decades: five-year plans are too short, fifty-year plans too long. What do people think about a subvention? Is it effective? Ineffective? Any thoughts? If you give it a name and make it a prize to help someone publish their first book—they have to have a contract, but many times presses can veto pictures—and so many people need visual material. We know the cost of permissions can be prohibitive. . . . I mean, what can *we* do? I know in the digital age, you can put a lot of material up online. Right, Connie?

SCHULZ: You have to have all the same permissions.

CLINTON: Well, there are some work-arounds . . .

SCHULZ: A lot of people don't get those permissions . . .

CLINTON: There is one work around, for example, if you are doing a book and you have illustrations for articles you are reprinting, if you have a URL direct link to that article (not behind a paywall), then you don't have to pay permission for the illustration.

Another pennysaver, having a party at the SHA and you want to have a nice cake, some coffee, and spend less than four hundred dollars: you can bring your own cake if it has a picture on it, because the hotel doesn't do picture cakes at hotels . . . [laughter in background] . . . But, guess what, if you put even *your own* book cover on a cake at a Publix or Piggly-Wiggly, they require permission . . . [more laughter] . . . from the publisher. Luckily I could run back to the book exhibit and get a signature, so think of the tricks . . . we are working in a very visual age. Glenda, I would like for you to repeat for the record what you were explaining to the graduate students about their web pages at their own universities, promoting dissertations, promoting themselves.

GILMORE: I mentioned earlier that I look at so many history department websites. When graduate students don't have their own photograph up . . . just one of those egg things! Nor a good explanation about what they are working on, what their peers do. As much as we may dislike it, self-promotion is really going to be important. If you don't want to do it for yourself, do it for your work. It's like you take care of your child. . . . you get out there, and that's what Keisha Blain did with her book. She got out and said, "I think these women are great and I want you to know about them, too." That's the way you should start, as a graduate student promoting yourself. And, the SAWH has a twitter account? [Crowd affirms]

WALKER: And a Facebook page.

GILMORE: Okay, with which I have not been trusted yet. [laughter]

SOMEONE IN THE CROWD: You can always hashtag. [laughter from the crowd]

GILMORE: We should always promote our members' books, you know, it's just everything takes so much time.

JONES-BRANCH: Put it at the bottom of your email. That's what I do. I put my most recent book and what's in progress. You know, every time I look at it, I know what I need [laughter in background], I mean, there are tricks to the trade. [crosstalk]

CLINTON: Well, on that note, we all have places to go, things to do, much to get done. But we want to thank the audience here for today. [applause] And see you next year at the SAWH. We'll all be in Louisville to celebrate the Milbauer Professor as the next president of the SHA. And then, on to Memphis for the fiftieth anniversary in 2020, with Thavolia Glymph at the helm.[13]

Cheers. [applause]

Notes

1. Bryant Simon, "The Appeal of Cole Blease of South Carolina: Race, Class, and Sex in the New South," *Journal of Southern History* 62, no. 1 (1996): 57–86.

2. John Howard, *Men Like That: A Southern Queer History* (Chicago: University of Chicago Press, 1999).

3. E. Patrick Johnson, *Sweet Tea: Gay Black Men of the South: An Oral History* (Chapel Hill: University of North Carolina Press, 2008).

4. Stephanie McCurry, *Masters of Small Worlds: Yeoman Households, Gender Relations, and the Political Culture of the Antebellum South Carolina Low Country* (New York: Oxford University Press, 1995).

5. Keri Leigh Merritt, *Masterless Men: Poor Whites and Slavery in the Antebellum South* (New York: Cambridge University Press, 2017).

6. Bradley Proctor, "'The K. K. Alphabet': Secret Communication and Coordination of the Reconstruction-Era Ku Klux Klan in the Carolinas," *Journal of the Civil War Era* 8, no. 3 (September 2018): 455–87.

7. Crystal N. Feimster, *Southern Horrors: Women and the Politics of Rape and Lynching* (Cambridge, Mass.: Harvard University Press, 2009).

8. Beth English, "'I have . . . a lot of work to do': Cotton Mill Work and Women's Culture in Matoaca, Virginia, 1888–95," *Virginia Magazine of History and Biography* 114, no. 3 (2006): 356–83.

9. Laurel Thatcher Ulrich, *A Midwife's Tale: The Life of Martha Ballard, Based on Her Diary, 1785–1812* (New York: Alfred A. Knopf, 1990).

10. Robin Copp Schulz, Mary Sherrer, Nicollette Calhoun, Peggy Clark, Taylor Kirton, Rachel Love, Justin McIntyre, Neal Millikan, and Benjamin Sheinkin, eds., *The Papers of Eliza Lucas Pinckney and Harriott Pinckney Horry: Digital Edition* (Charlottesville, Va.: Rotunda, 2012), found online at https://src6.cas.sc.edu/poelp/welcome.

11. For more information, contact Michelle Krowl: mkrowl@loc.gov.

12. Erica Armstrong Dunbar, *Never Caught: The Washingtons' Relentless Pursuit of Their Runaway Slave, Ona Judge* (New York: Simon & Schuster, 2017); Tiya Miles, *The Dawn of Detroit: A Chronicle of Slavery and Freedom in the City of the Straits* (New York: New Press, 2017).

13. Although in-person events for the 2020 SHA conference and SAWH Fiftieth Anniversary were cancelled due to COVID-19, Jacquelyn Dowd Hall offered an online address as part of the virtual sessions.

Appendix B

Southern Association for Women Historians
List of Presidents, 1970–2020

1970–1972	Charlotte M. Davis	Cochair
	Mollie C. Davis	Cochair
1973–1974	Constance Ashton Myers	
1975	Arnita Jones	
1976	Rosemary Carroll	
1977	Helena Lewis	
1978	Martha Swain	

Session "Documenting Southern History," Carolyn A. Wallace on holdings at University of North Carolina, Chapel Hill. Elizabeth Jacoway on holdings at University of Arkansas, Little Rock.

1979	Judith Gentry

A. Elizabeth Taylor, "The History of Southern Women: An Appraisal and Some Suggestions."

1980	Carol Bleser (Tenth Anniversary of SAWH)

Session "Three Women Presidents of the Southern Historical Association: Ella Lonn, Kathryn Trimmer, Mary Elizabeth Massey," LaWanda Cox, Blanche Henry Clark Weaver, and Frederick Heath. (This was a session titled "Three Women Presidents of the Southern Historical Association." Cox presented on Lonn, Weaver on Trimmer, Heath on Massey. Papers were published in Spring 1981 of *Southern Studies*.)

1981	Elizabeth Jacoway

Anne Firor Scott, "The Biography of an Idea."

1982	Jo Ann Carrigan

A. Elizabeth Taylor, LaWanda Cox, and Mollie Davis, "Women's Issues: Report and Inquiry by the Committee on the Status of Women, Southern Historical Association."

1983   Betty Brandon

Darlene Clark Hine, "Lifting the Veil, Shattering the Silence: Black Women's History in Slavery and Freedom."[1]

1984   Margaret Ripley Wolfe

Tom Appleton and Nancy Baird, "Vignettes of Kentucky Women."

1985   Darlene Clark Hine

Barbara J. Fields, "Ideology and the Writing of Southern History,"

1986   Theda Perdue

Mary Frederickson, "Sassing Fate: Women Workers in the Twentieth-Century South."

1987   Joanne V. Hawks

Joan E. Cashin, "Women's Work and Culture in the Old Southwest."

1988   Judith Jennings

Suzanne Lebsock, "White Supremacy and Woman Suffrage: A Virginia Case Study."

1989   Virginia Bernhard

Barbara Welter, "The True Woman: Post-Feminist or Retro-Feminist?"

1990   Julia Blackwelder

Catherine Clinton, "Sex and the Sectional Conflict."

1991   Marlene Rikard

Virginia van der Veer Hamilton, "Clio's Daughters: Whence and Whither?"

1992   Connie Schulz

Theda Perdue, "Pochahontas Meets Columbus in the American South."

1993   Elsa Barkley Brown

Thavolia Glymph, "Civil War Memoirs and the Reinvention of Black Women's History."

1994   Janet Coryell

Jean B. Lee, "Experiencing the American Revolution."

1995   Kathleen Berkeley

Anne Firor Scott, "Unfinished Business . . ."
1996   Marjorie Spruill Wheeler

Glenda Elizabeth Gilmore, "'But She Can't Find Her (V.O.) Key': Writing Gender and Race into Southern Political History."
1997   Elizabeth Hayes Turner

Darlene Clark Hine, "A Stronger Soul Within a Finer Frame: Writing a Literary History of Black Women."
1998   Catherine Clinton

Jacquelyn Dowd Hall, "Writing a Way Home: History, Memory, and the Refashioning of Southern Identity."
1999   Drew Faust

Stephanie McCurry, "'The Brothers' War'?: Free Women, Slaves, and Popular Politics in the Civil War 'South.'"
2000   Amy Thompson McCandless

Nancy A. Hewitt, "Seneca Falls, Suffrage, and the South: Remapping the Landscape of Women's Rights in America, 1848–1965."
2001   Jacqueline A. Rouse

Rosalyn Terborg-Penn, "The ABWH, Black Women's History, and Black Women Historians."
2002   Sandra Gioia Treadway

Jane Dailey, "Sex, Segregation, and the Sacred from Brown to Selma."
2003   Jane Turner Censer

Marjorie Julian Spruill, "Countdown to Houston: The 1977 IWY Conferences and the Polarization of American Women."
2004   Stephanie Cole

Grace Elizabeth Hale, "The Southern Black Roots of Postwar American Culture and Politics, or the Strange Career of the White Negro."
2005   Michele Gillespie

Jacqueline Jones, "Nancy Johnson's Story: Rethinking the History of Women in the South During the Civil War and Reconstruction."
2006   Glenda Gilmore

Anne Firor Scott, "Reading Other People's Mail."
2007   Cynthia Kierner

Michele Gillespie, "Making Herself Modern: Katharine Smith Reynolds and the New South."

2008   Laura Edwards

Sandra Treadway, "Pioneers to Power Brokers: Women Office Holders in Twentieth-Century Virginia."

2009   Melissa Walker

Rebecca Sharpless, "Remembering Past One Another: Idella Parker, Marjorie Kinnan Rawlings, and Autobiography at Cross Creek."

2010   Jane Dailey

Heather Ann Thompson, "Redemption Redux? Southern Politics, Economy, and Society in the Age of Mass Incarceration."

2011   Sally McMillen

Elizabeth Hayes Turner, "'To Help Our Nation Find Its Soul': Women and the 1968 Poor People's Campaign."

2012   Beverly Bond

Crystal Feimster, "'Indecent and Obscene': White Officers, Black Women, and Rape in the 'Contraband Quarters' of the American Civil War."

2013   Rebecca Sharpless

LaShonda Mims, "Drastic Dykes: The New South and Lesbian Life from Hotlanta to the Queen City."

2014   Emily Clark

Jennifer L. Morgan, "'Partus Sequitur Ventrum': Colonial Slave Law and the History of Women in Slavery."

2015   Lorri Glover

Anya Jabour, "The Making of a Southern Feminist: Sophonisba Preston Breckinridge."

2016   Angela Boswell

Cherisse Jones-Branch, "'Been a Guinea Pig in This Race': Annie R. Zachary, Arkansas Homemaker, Farmer, and Politician."

2017   Megan Taylor Shockley

Cynthia A. Kierner, "Awful Calamity: Sentiment, Gender, and the Nation in the Richmond Theater Fire of 1811."

2018   Barbara Krauthamer

Kendra Field, "'Thoughts to Be Forgotten': African American Family History and Silences after Emancipation."

2019   Janet Allured

Anne Sarah Rubin, "'I Can't Buy One Mouth Full of Nothing to Eat': Women and the Struggle for Sustenance in the Civil War South"

2020   Jennifer Ritterhouse

Note

1. Betty Brandon, "The Forty-Ninth Annual Meeting," *Journal of Southern History* 50, no. 1 (February 1984): 97–98. Brandon writes, "In the absence of the scheduled speaker, Thavolia Glymph of the University of Texas at Arlington, who was unable to attend because of a family emergency, Darlene Clark Hine of Purdue University presented 'Lifting the Veil, Shattering the Silence: Black Women's History in Slavery and Freedom,' a provocative review of research in progress and additional subjects to investigate in the field of black women's history."

Appendix C

University of Missouri Press

Southern Women Series

Hidden Histories of Women in the New South (1994)
ed. Virginia Bernhard, Betty Brandon, Elizabeth Fox-Genovese, Theda Perdue, and Elizabeth Hayes Turner

Beyond Image and Convention: Explorations in Southern Women's History (1998)
ed. Janet L. Coryell, Martha H. Swain, Sandra Gioia Treadway, and Elizabeth Hayes Turner

Taking Off the White Gloves: Southern Women and Women Historians (1998)
ed. Michele Gillespie and Catherine Clinton

Negotiating Boundaries of Southern Womanhood: Dealing with the Powers That Be (2000)
ed. Janet L. Coryell, Thomas H. Appleton, Anastatia Sims, and Sandra Gioia Treadway

Searching for Their Places: Women in the South across Four Centuries (2003)
ed. Thomas H. Appleton and Angela Boswell

Clio's Southern Sisters: Interviews with Leaders of the Southern Association for Women Historians (2004)
ed. Constance B. Schulz and Elizabeth Hayes Turner

Women Shaping the South: Creating and Confronting Change (2006)
ed. Angela Boswell and Judith N. McArthur

Entering the Fray: Gender, Politics, and Culture in the New South (2009)
ed. Jonathan Daniel Wells and Sheila R. Phipps

Contributors

CATHERINE CLINTON (A.B. Harvard, M.A. Sussex, Ph.D. Princeton) is the Denman Endowed Chair of American History at the University of Texas in San Antonio and an emerita professor at Queen's University Belfast, where she held a chair in U.S. History from 2006 to 2014. She is the author and editor of more than two dozen books, including *The Plantation Mistress: Woman's World in the Old South*; *Tara Revisited: Women, War and the Plantation Legend*; *Fanny Kemble's Civil Wars*; *Harriet Tubman: The Road to Freedom*; and *Mrs. Lincoln: A Life*. Her first book for young readers, *I, Too, Sing America: Three Centuries of African American Poetry*, won the Bank Street Poetry Prize in 1998. She has served as a consultant on several film projects, including Steven Spielberg's *Lincoln* (2012). She delivered the Fleming Lectures at LSU, published as *Stepdaughters of History: Southern Women and the American Civil War*. She was awarded a Guggenheim Fellowship in 2016 for her ongoing work on Union soldiers and mental illness, during and after the Civil War. In 2019, she edited the first volume in her new coedited series, *History in the Headlines: Confederate Statues and Memorialization*. She is a past president of both the Southern Historical Association and the Southern Association for Women Historians.

MICHELE GILLESPIE (B.A. Rice University, Ph.D. Princeton) is Presidential Endowed Chair of Southern History and dean of the College at Wake Forest University. She is the author of *Katharine and R. J. Reynolds: Partners of Fortune in the Making of the New South*, named a CHOICE Outstanding Academic Title, and *Free Labor in an Unfree World: White Artisans in Slaveholding* Georgia, winner of the Malcolm and Muriel Bell Award for Most Distinguished Book in Georgia History. She coedited the two-volume *North Carolina Women: Their Lives and Times*; the three-volume New Directions in the History of Southern Economy and Society series; *Pious Pursuits: German Moravians in the Atlantic World*; *Thomas Dixon and the Birth of Modern America*; *Neither Lady Nor Slave: Working Women of the Old South*; *Taking Off the White Gloves: Southern*

Women and Women's History; and *The Devil's Lane: Sex and Race in the Early South*. She is the author of a dozen articles on the gendered politics, changing technologies, and racial realities of artisanal and working-class men and women in the nineteenth-century South and is coeditor of the New Directions in Southern History series at the University Press of Kentucky. She is a past president and past secretary of the Southern Association for Women Historians.

GLENDA ELIZABETH GILMORE is the Peter V. and C. Vann Woodward Professor of History Emeritus at Yale University. She was also a member of the African American Studies and American Studies Departments. She earned her Ph.D. at the University of North Carolina at Chapel Hill. In 2018 and 2019, she was the Mary Ball Washington Visiting Chair in American History at University College Dublin. She is the author of several award-winning books and articles, including *Gender and Jim Crow: Women and the Politics of White Supremacy in North Carolina, 1896–1920* and *Defying Dixie: The Radical Roots of Civil Rights*. She has received fellowships from the Guggenheim Foundation, the National Endowment for the Humanities, the Radcliffe Institute, and the American Council of Learned Societies, among others. Her current book project is *Bearden's Collage: The Saga of an African American Family from Slavery to Civil Rights*.

CHERISSE JONES-BRANCH is the James and Wanda Lee Vaughn Endowed Professor of History and the director of the ASTATE Digital Press at Arkansas State University. She teaches courses in U.S. history, women's history, civil rights history, rural history, African American history, and heritage studies. Jones-Branch received her bachelors and masters degrees from the College of Charleston, South Carolina, and a doctorate in history from Ohio State University, Columbus. She has been teaching at Arkansas State University since 2003. Jones-Branch has authored numerous articles on women's civil rights and rural activism. She published *Crossing the Line: Women and Interracial Activism in South Carolina during and after World War II* and coedited *Arkansas Women: Their Lives and Times*. She is currently revising a second monograph, *Better Living By Their Own Bootstraps: Rural Black Women's Activism in Arkansas*.

MELISSA WALKER is the Emerita George Dean Johnson, Jr. Professor of History at Converse College, where she taught for twenty-one years. She began her career working in institutional advancement before earning her Ph.D. in U.S. and women's history at Clark University. Her research has focused on women's history and labor history. She is the author or editor of nine books, including *All We Knew Was to Farm: Rural Women in the Upcountry South, 1919–1941*, which received the Willie Lee Rose Prize from the SAWH, and *Southern Farmers and Their Stories: Memory and Meaning in Oral History*. In 2007, she was honored by CASE and the Carnegie Foundation for Teaching with the South Carolina Professor of the Year Award. She served as both executive secretary and president of the SAWH. She is the founder of Heyday Coaching, a personal and career coaching firm that specializes in working with academics. The business takes its name from Elizabeth Cady Stanton's assertion that "fifty, not fifteen is the heyday of life."

Index

Page numbers in *italics* refer to tables.

Welter, Barbara, 128

West, Tim, 26

White, Deborah Gray, 66, 77

Whites, LeeAnn, 41, 46, 52

Wilkerson-Freeman, Sarah, 79

William and Mary University Libraries, 27

Williamson, Joel, 91

Willie Lee Rose Prize, 2, 65, 95, 98, 107; awardees, 3, 8–9, 28, 98–99; controversy over, 3, 18n23, 19n27, 118

Wilson Special Collections Library (UNC Chapel Hill), 18n23, 19n27, 26–27

Winthrop College, 2

Wolfe, Margaret Ripley, 63, 128

Women Military Aviators Digital Archive (Texas Woman's University), 11

Women's Equity Action League, 63

Women's history. *See* African American women's history; Feminism; Southern white women's history

Women's Home and Foreign Missionary Society of the African Methodist Episcopal Zion Church, 78

Women's Rights National Historical Park, 50

Woodward, C. Vann, 6–7, 38, 90, 91, 96

Wooley, Mary, 72n3

Woolf, Virginia, 39–40

Yale University, 22, 105, 120

Yale University Press, 95

Yanchisin, Daniel, 27

Young Women's Christian Association, 78